MAKING CHEESE, BUTTER, CREAM AND YOGURT

A practical guide to home dairying, describing the techniques for producing cheeses, butters, cream and yogurt and including a selection of suggested recipes.

By the same author
YOUR OWN DAIRY COW

MAKING CHEESES, BUTTERS, CREAM AND YOGURT AT HOME

How to Make the Most of Your Milk Supply

by
Patricia Cleveland-Peck

THORSONS PUBLISHERS LIMITED
Wellingborough, Northamptonshire

First published 1980

© PATRICIA CLEVELAND-PECK 1980

This book is sold subject to the condition that it shall not, by way of trade or otherwise, be lent, re-sold, hired out, or otherwise circulated without the publisher's prior consent in any form of binding or cover other than that in which it is published and without a similar condition including this condition being imposed on the subsequent purchaser.

British Library Cataloguing in Publication Data

Cleveland-Peck, Patricia
   Making cheeses, butters, cream and yogurt at home.
   1. Dairy products
   I. Title
   637   SF239

ISBN 0-7225-0596-5
ISBN 0-7225-0597-3 Pbk

Photoset by Specialised Offset Services Limited, Liverpool
and printed in Great Britain by
Weatherby Woolnough, Wellingborough, Northamptonshire
on paper made from 100% re-cycled fibre supplied by
P.F. Bingham Limited, Croydon, Surrey

CONTENTS

		Page
	Introduction	9
Chapter		
1.	Milk	11
2.	Milk Recipes	28
3.	Yogurt	39
4.	Cream	47
5.	Butter	63
6.	Cheese-making: The Technique	78
7.	Cheese-making Recipes	96
	Useful Addresses	121
	Further Reading	123
	Index	125

To my son Justin who enjoys both
farming and eating

ACKNOWLEDGEMENT

I would like to thank Mr J.A.W. Todd, Dairy Husbandry Advisory Officer with the Ministry of Agriculture for his help and advice. I would also like to thank Mrs E.A.D. May of Priestlands Goat Farm, Kent for advice and permission to quote her recipe for Halloumi and Anari cheese.

Finally I would like to thank my husband Dennis (fortunately for me a trained caterer before turning smallholder) for his help in trying out some of the recipes included here.

AUTHOR'S NOTE

Although it is preferable from the point of view of finance to have a fresh-from-the-farm supply of milk for making butters and cheeses at home it is possible to use the bottled pasteurized milk that the milkman leaves on your doorstep. Avoid using sterilized or UHT milk, though, as the high temperatures to which these have been subjected would inhibit the rennet action in cheese-making.

INTRODUCTION

Milk is one of the most versatile of foods. When fresh it provides an invigorating drink and an essential accompaniment to breakfast cereals, and when cooked it adds taste and texture to everything it encounters. It can be separated into cream, the ultimate luxury food, while at the same time providing a useful by-product in the form of skimmed milk. The cream can further be converted into butter, making our bread more palatable and enhancing our culinary creations as well as yielding another useful by-product, buttermilk. As if this were not enough, by a different process milk can be transformed into cheese (with the by-product whey) and can be thus preserved for weeks, months or even years. An impressive variety of cheeses can be produced; soft, hard, flaky, crumbly, bland, strong or subtle. They differ so vastly in every way that one could eat a different cheese every day for many years without becoming bored or having to sample the same one twice. All from milk.

If, therefore you have your own milk supply from a house cow or goat you are very fortunate, for you have a ready supply of this most nourishing food. Indeed, if you had to choose one substance on which to live it would be hard to rival milk; a fact appreciated by the Masai and Borana tribes of Africa whose diet is almost exclusively milk, with the occasional meat feast.

Milk is produced by all mammals but the milk used in dairying in this country is supplied by the cow, the goat and to a lesser extent by the milk sheep.

This book assumes you have a ready supply of milk. For this reason I do not propose to deal with the breeds of cattle or goats or the quality or quantity of yields. There are books and pamphlets available on these subjects (see *Suggested Further Reading*) to which anyone proposing to acquire a dairy animal can turn for guidance. My aim here is to help you to make the best use of your milk supply. I hope to explain the basic dairying techniques in simple terms, illustrated and with instructions and recipes where relevant.

1

MILK

Although animals have been milked by man almost from the dawn of civilization (Egyptian paintings show cattle being milked around 3000 BC) the use of liquid milk was almost unknown until comparatively recently. Until the beginning of the seventeenth century milk drinking was considered quite injurious to health and, in view of the low standards of dairy hygiene, the incidence of cattle plague and the fact that milk contained dangerous pathogenic factors, especially the germs of tuberculosis and typhoid, this was probably right. Many, many children died of tuberculosis of bovine origin up until the late nineteenth century and it was not until the 1930s when pasteurization and refrigeration of milk became accepted and when concentrated efforts were inaugurated to eradicate the disease of bovine tuberculosis, that milk drinking became safe and acceptable.

Composition of Milk

Milk is one of the most complete foods. It contains all the food factors and three of its constituents, fat, casein and lactose are found in no other food.

Older books refer to the structure of milk as consisting of three substances, the caseous, the buytrose and the serous. The first consists of the particles of carbonate of lime which when artificially coagulated form cheese, and which serve to suspend the second element, the buytrose. This is in fact the cream, butterfat or oily particles which float to the surface and when agitated, become butter. The third is the watery part which becomes the whey.

The total solids of milk can be divided into fats, i.e. butterfat, and non-fat solids, i.e. all the remaining constituents.

Fats

The fat of milk is extremely complex and contains some sixty fatty acids. It has the highest commercial value of all and the proportion of fat contained is the main measure of the milk's quality. This is measured as butterfat percentage. The butterfat is in the form of globules which float in the milk and are easily separated from the rest.

Some breeds of cattle and some individual cattle produce milk of larger globules but in all cases the globules become smaller as the lactation advances.

The larger globules float to the surface and are more suitable for butter-making. Milk with smaller globules however, is more digestible. It is for this reason that goat's milk in which the globules are very small indeed, although the overall butterfat content is high, is often used for children or people with weak digestions.

Generally in cattle the higher the yield, the lower the butterfat content. During the lactation the butterfat content drops at first and then rises throughout the lactation.

	Fat	Protein	Lactose	Minerals	Water
Cow	3.73	3.58	4.90	0.71	87.08
Goat	4.78	4.29	4.46	0.76	85.71
Ewe	6.86	6.52	4.91	0.89	80.82

Figure 1. Composition of various milks

The composition of milk varies greatly depending on the stage of the actual milking.

	Fat	Protein	Total solids	Water
First quart	1.20	3.70	10.58	89.42
Last 2	7.88	3.48	16.63	83.37
Strippings	10.00	3.37	19.40	80.60

Figure 2. Composition of milk at each stage of milking

This indicates how essential it is to milk out thoroughly, and also that if you share the milk with a calf, taking your share first and leaving him to finish, he does by far the best from the point of view of rich creamy milk!

Non-fat Solids

These are all the remaining constituents and can be subdivided into the following categories.

Proteins

Casein is the main milk protein. It is this which gives the milk its white colour and which coagulates when sour. The little white flecks which form on slightly sour milk are casein. Prior to plastics, casein was

MILK

used extensively in various manufacturing processes e.g. buttonmaking. It is now dried and used as 'creamer' for tea and coffee, as well as for making paint and glue.

Albumin and globulin are also present in smaller quantities. The milk proteins are sometimes known as albuminoids.

Lactose
This is the milk sugar. It is not as sweet as cane or beet sugars but has a beneficial action on the intestines.

Minerals
Minerals are natural substances contained in the earth's structure, they are absorbed by the plants which in turn are eaten by the animals. Thus ingested they occur in minute quantities in milk and are of the greatest importance to the bone development and general health of young animals. They include calcium, phosphorus, potassium and iron.

Vitamins
Milk contains all the thirteen known vitamins. Colostrum, the first milk yielded by a mammal immediately after giving birth, contains about ten times as much vitamin A (the anti-infective vitamin) as normal milk. All these vitamins are contained in the most minute quantities, all the vitamin D from 23 gallons (115 litres) of milk would just cover a pin head.

Water
Water acts as the suspending agent and is of no more chemical value than any other type of water.

Types of Cow's Milk
The dairy industry designates several types of milk for legislative purposes.

Untreated Milk
This is simply raw milk filtered and cooled prior to bottling. The vitamin content of this milk is slightly higher than heat-treated milk. It is commercially identified by the green top.

14 MAKING CHEESES, BUTTERS, CREAM AND YOGURT

Pasteurized Milk
This is milk which has been subjected to a specific form of heat treatment (see page 16) which wipes out the pathogenic or disease-bearing bacteria. 80-90 per cent of the vitamin content remains the same and is identified by the silver top.

Homogenized Milk
This is milk heated to reduce surface tension and then forced at high pressure through very small holes to reduce the globules to a size at which they no longer rise. There is no cream line and the milk is very easy to digest because of these small globules and the soft curd formation which occurs as they are digested. It is identified by the red top.

Channel Island and South Devon
This is milk from the Jersey, Guernsey and south Devon breeds of cattle with a minimum fat content of four per cent. It is available both untreated and pasteurized. The high butterfat content makes for a delicious creamy taste. Untreated it is identified by a green top with a single gold stripe; pasteurized it has the gold top.

Sterilized Milk
This is milk which has been subjected to a process which destroys bacteria more completely than any other. The milk is pre-heated, homogenized and put into bottles sealed with an air tight seal. The bottles are then subjected to a temperature of 219°-230°F (104°-110°C) in autoclaves for 30-40 minutes. They are cooled naturally. There is an alternative continuous process where they pass through steam chambers and water cooling tanks. This type of milk has excellent keeping properties but the caramelization of the lactose gives it a different flavour from fresh milk and the vitamin and food values are also reduced.

Ultra Heat Treated Milk
This type of milk has the best keeping qualities of all. It has gone through a process whereby it has been held at a temperature of 270°F (132°C) for one second and is then packed under sterile conditions in special foil-lined containers. It is known as long-life milk and is useful for camping and travelling.

Condensed Milk
This is milk mixed with sugar and heated to 235°F (112°C) and condensed in a vacuum to two fifths of its original volume.

Evaporated Milk
This is milk evaporated in a vacuum pan at 130°-140°F (55-60°C) and reduced to half its volume. The process causes the formation of fine curds which make the milk easy to digest.

Dried Milks
Any type of milk can be dried and there is now a good market for dried skimmed milk amongst weight-watchers.

Goat's and Ewe's Milk
Neither the goat nor the ewe are recognized as dairy animals in the same way as cows in Britain. This leads to some strange anomalies, one of the most obvious being that the products of these animals are easier to market as they are not covered by the stringent regulations which apply to the sale of the dairy products of the cow. The Ministry of Agriculture however, is aware of these anomalies, which came into being during the last war when goats were classed with poultry and rabbits as small animals and delegated to a different Husbandry Officer from the dairy animals. I cannot see it being too long before dairy animals are redefined for legislative purposes. Moves may also be made to restrict sales from the farm gate, yet this however has always been a farmer's prerogative and smallholders especially should fight to retain that right.

The constituents of the milk of goats and ewes are the same as that of cow's milk but in different proportions. The flavour is thus altered although, if the animals are well housed and hygienically kept the milk is no less sweet and fresh tasting – just different.

Souring
As well as the constituents mentioned above milk contains millions of bacteria, many of them beneficial. Milk sours when these naturally occurring bacteria convert some of the lactose in the milk into lactic acid. In simple terms this means that the lactose goes with the albumin and globulin particles (and the B vitamins) into the whey, leaving the casein which entangles nearly all the milk fat particles and phosphates as a coagulum, or curd. More will be said about this process later, as it

is of the greatest relevance in cheese-making.

Sour milk becomes bad milk if the milk continues to be broken down and the bacteria multiply beyond a certain point. At this point the acidity disappears and the medium becomes alkaline and putrid. Once started these chemical changes take place very rapidly. Temperature plays an important part in the speed at which they occur and an understanding of them is a fundamental requirement of dairying.

Pasteurization

Most milk sold commercially is subjected to the process of pasteurization which successfully kills the pathogenic or disease-bearing bacteria without either ridding the milk of all its micro-organisms or destroying the vitamin content. The French scientist Louis Pasteur discovered this process when studying fermentation in wine in the 1860's but it was not fully applied to milk until recently because when first used it denatured the protein and mineral element in the milk and altered it so that for example rennet would not coagulate it for cheese-making. Later the process was perfected and now all milk is pasteurized and then inoculated with various 'starters', that is, strong doses of the bacteria required for the specific purpose of cheese-making or butter-making.

If however, pasteurized milk goes off, it should be rejected because as the pasteurizing process removes most of the lactic acid bacteria, the souring is invariably caused by other bacteria which can be harmful.

For the home producer pasteurization is not of importance in milk production (although heat-treatment and inoculation with a starter is important in cheese-making). Provided the animal is healthy, cleanly milked and the milk is filtered and cooled there is rarely any need to put it through this process. Goat's milk sold in the U.K. is never pasteurized. There is however a home pasteurizer on the market (see *Useful Addresses*).

Methods of Pasteurization

There are two methods of pasteurization. In the first, the Holder method, milk is heated to 145-150°F (63-66°C), held there for 30 minutes and then cooled immediately. In the second, the high temperature method, the milk is heated to 161°F (72°C) kept there for 20 seconds and cooled immediately to 50°F (10°C).

MILK

What Gives Milk its Character?

Colour
Milk is basically white but most samples have a yellow tinge. The deeper the yellow the creamier it is thought to be and the higher market value it has. Yellow colour is associated with fat and is derived from carotene which is converted from the chlorophyll in green forages, from carrots, yellow corn and fresh hay. Weathered hay and bleached pastures are deficient in it.

The factors which influence the degree of colouring are:
Butterfat content. As carotene is associated with fat, milk having a greater proportion of butterfat dispersed through it bears a deeper colour than milk produced under the same feeding and housing conditions but with less butterfat.
Feeding. Cows fed on green food obviously ingest more chlorophyll and therefore make more carotene than those fed on cereals and roots. Summer milk is, accordingly, deeper in colour.
Breed. The main reason however, is undoubtedly genetic. Jersey, Guernsey and south Devon breeds as well as individual cows will produce richer coloured milk than others. The skin and fat of these animals is also yellow. The reason for this is that these cows do not convert the carotene into vitamin A as do the 'white milk' breeds. The yellow fat types store the carotene without converting it and pass it on to the consumer either in the milk or in the meat fat, leaving him to convert it to vitamin A within his own body. Other elements being equal there is no nutritional value difference between white and yellow milk but it is firmly entrenched in the public taste to prefer yellow milk to white (and white fat to yellow!). In the same way they prefer brown eggs to white without there being any rational explanation for this preference.

Flavour in Milk
Goat's milk is slightly sweeter than cows' milk. This said, of course one must qualify it, some goat's milk is sweeter than some cow's milk. The taste does vary from individual to individual and from stage to stage in the lactation. As the animal nears the end of her lactation the lactose content falls and the chloride content rises giving the milk a slightly saltier taste. This salty taste can also be a sign of mastitis so beware if it occurs at any other stage.

Taints in Milk

Milk is the ideal substance for the development of taints i.e. unusual flavours or smells other than normal souring, for the following reasons:

1. It is an excellent medium for the rapid growth of bacteria, some of which themselves cause taints to develop.
2. It lends itself to absorbing flavour from strong smelling substances around it.
3. Its chemical constituents change very rapidly.

If taints occur which are not readily identifiable they are usually bacteriological. A characteristic of these taints is that they are not noticeable at milking but develop quickly if the ambient temperature is high. In an effort to define them they are given descriptive names such as, 'mouldy', 'fruity', 'caramelly' or 'fishy'. In the event of this happening all equipment should be examined and given a thorough cleaning, the cow should be given extra cleaning too, especially the udder. The milk should also be very rapidly cooled.

Milk from sick animals can be tainted either from the illness itself (most evident in the case of acetonaemia, when the cow and her milk give off a strong smell of peardrops in an attempt by the animal to rid her system of excess acetone) or by the drugs which she is being given to cure an illness.

Sometimes something known as 'spontaneous rancidity' occurs towards the end of a cow's lactation, this has to do with the action of lipase, a lipolytic or fat-splitting enzyme, which causes a rancid taste which develops after cooling and becomes very noticeable after storage. This also causes the 'goaty' taste in some goat's milk.

'Oxidative rancidity' is another condition which has been described as giving the milk a 'cardboardy' or 'tallowy' taste. This is found occasionally in milk containing few bacteria which has been stored at a low temperature.

Absorbed Taints

Certain bulky foods such as cabbage, kale, clover, roots or beet tops may taint the milk and should therefore be fed immediately after milking. Certain weeds which the animal can pick up herself e.g. wild onion, ransoms, hedge mustard, yarrow, stinking mayweed, may also bring it about. With the exception of stinking mayweed these tainting agents do not persist if the weed is made into hay. Some organic farmers believe that if the cow is free to browse on hedgerow herbs she will do herself a lot of good. Newman Turner in his famous book *Herdsmanship* (see *Suggested Further Reading*) advocates the inclusion of some of these herbs, especially ransoms, in the cow's diet, although he does emphasize that the quantities necessary for maintaining health are not sufficient to taint the milk.

Non-Food Absorptions
The odours from paint, disinfectant, tar, turps, paraffin and strong smelling foodstuffs can be absorbed by milk and it should not therefore be exposed to such atmospheres. Hands should not be washed with carbolic soaps because of the danger of phenolic tainting.

Goat's Milk
All that has gone before on the subject of taints applies equally to all types of milk but the milk of the goat has a few problems all of its own. A controversy still does exist as to whether goat's milk has a special 'goaty' taste, and if so what causes it. Some people claim that it has and that they loathe it, others that it has and they like it! At the same time many people (myself included) have drunk plenty of goat's milk without noticing the difference. If a goat is in good health, cleanly housed and hygienically milked there is no reason why the milk should not taste sweet and fresh. If it does not the fault may be traced to something like the 'spontaneous rancidity' mentioned above. Rancidity is caused when the lipolyic enzymes, mainly lipase, react with the fat in the milk to form free fatty acids. Some of these acids (and there are some sixty in milk) have an unpleasant rancid taste and may impart this 'goat' flavour. It would seem that some goats produce more lipase than others and this may be a genetic characteristic.

Clean Milk Production
Contamination starts the instant your milk leaves the cow, goat or ewe. Having spent time and money on your animal it is worth spending just a little extra time and thought on obtaining and preserving your milk in optimum condition. Cleanliness is absolutely fundamental to this and at the risk of being boring and repetitive I shall say so at every stage of dairying I mention.

Milking Area
Right from the beginning of milk production you should have a good clean place to milk your animal. It should be cool, dirt and dust free

and it should be possible to hose it down. Warm straw-filled boxes are cosy for your animals but also for the millions of bacteria which are just waiting to invade the milk. Your milking area need not be a model milking parlour, just a simple place other than where the animal sleeps.

It is thus possible to ensure that the animal herself is clean before she is brought to the milking area. Any muck should be cleaned off her and as a matter of routine she should be groomed (at least three times a week after morning milking) so that she is not for ever shedding hair. This is even more important in the case of goats whose hair is coarser and more easily shed. The loose hair around the udder should be well trimmed so that the long hairs which harbour dirt are eliminated and do not cause the animal pain by getting pulled during milking. Come to milk in a clean state yourself. While it is not absolutely necessary to put on a white coat to milk, although it is essential when working with milk in the dairy, you should make sure that long hair is tied back and that boots are free from muck. Commonsense indicates that a clean milking area is pointless if you yourself come in bearing millions of harmful bacteria. Your hands should be washed in disinfected water, your nails should be short and clean and the animals udder washed over with a warm sterile cloth. Not only does this remove surface dirt which might otherwise fall into your milking bucket, it also activates the let-down process.

All the equipment you use should be scrupulously clean. If you are hand-milking, this is quite simple. A stainless steel (milking only) bucket and a clean pair of hands are all you need. Stainless steel is the best material because it does not scratch and will not therefore harbour bacteria if kept clean. Such buckets are expensive and of course you can make do with plastic if you have to, but keep it extra clean. As a compromise there is a strong plastic 'Dairythene' bucket (see *Useful Addresses* for suppliers) which can be sterilized and is cheaper than stainless steel.

Fore-milk
The duct of the teat cannot be cleaned adequately by normal udder washing and therefore the first squirt of milk from each teat, which is also full of bacteria, may be contaminated by dirt. This first or fore-milk was traditionally given to the farm's cat but should as a precaution always be discarded. It should also be examined for any abnormalities such as clots or blood which may indicate mastitis. A

strip cup may be used; this is a device with a dark examination plate which shows up such abnormalities at the same time as serving as a receptacle for the fore-milk. A simple container equipped with a disk of black plastic can equally well be improvised. It is essential to examine the milk adequately as it will indicate signs of mastitis at an early stage, this is the most serious udder condition which threatens your milk supply and the health of your animal. If you are selling milk, this procedure is required by law.

Milk should be strained to remove any extraneous matter which has fallen in, either by a proper unit or through a piece of sterile muslin.

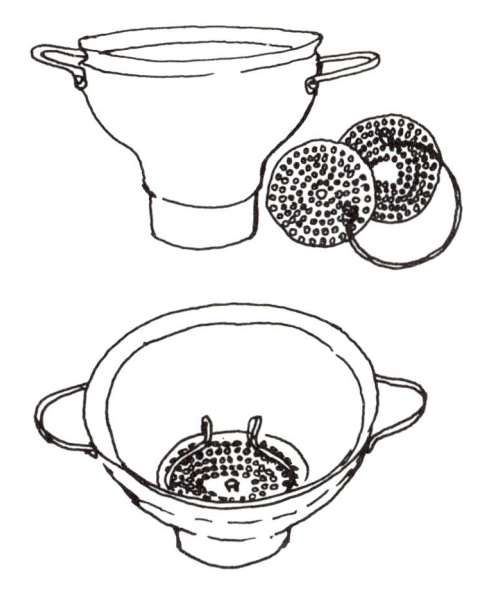

Figure 3. Milk strainer

If you are using a cream separator, you will run your milk through it warm from the cow. Otherwise the milk must be cooled rapidly to prevent deterioration. If you are using gallon churns, large sweet jars or any other container which you are placing directly in the fridge, stir or shake from time to time to ensure even cooling. A very satisfactory cooling collar can be made to fit over a churn's neck by perforating a circle of garden hose with a hot nail and joining this to the tap by means of a T-piece. If the churn is left standing in the sink and the water turned on so that it runs down the churn through the holes, effective cooling will take place.

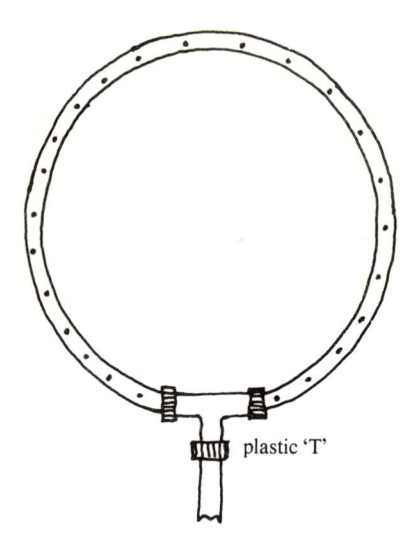

Figure 4. Churn cooler using hosepipe and plastic T

Cleaning of Dairy Equipment

All equipment must be thoroughly cleaned and sterilized before it comes into contact with milk again. There are several ways of doing this but they fall into 3 stages.

1 Cold wash out.
2 Sterilization – by boiling steaming or the use of a special product.
3 Final Rinse.

The cold wash removes the film from the surface of the equipment which can then be sterilized either by boiling (in e.g. a Burco boiler) or steaming for 10 minutes. Alternatively a proprietary hot detergent-sterilizer can be made up according to the manufacturer's instructions and the items immersed in it for the time stipulated. This must be followed by a cold rinse in clean water.

Milking Machines
If you milk by machine then the procedure is complicated by the fact that all the various pipes and surfaces need different brushes to clean them properly. This having been said the basic cleaning procedure above applies.

When you have tipped the milk out of your bucket, draw about 2 gallons (9 litres) of water through the clusters, lifting the cluster out of the water several times during the process to cause a surging action. Wash all remaining items, strainer, carrying bucket etc. and prepare your hot detergent-sterilizer, making it not less than 113°F (45°C) in temperature. Make up the chemical at the correct strength; there are powder, liquid and even jelly forms available. Further there are detergents, sterilizers and combined detergent-sterilizers which are obviously more useful.

If you are selling milk only boiling, steaming or the use of approved chemical sterilizers are permitted under the relevant regulations.

Because the teat-cup clusters are the most difficult to clean they are best dealt with first while the solution is at its hottest. To give them maximum contact time immerse all the clusters in the solution, detaching the long and short milk tubes from the claw piece to prevent air-locks. Brush each piece thoroughly with the appropriate brush allowing a contact time of 2 minutes then remove them for rinsing and immerse and brush bucket, lid, strainers etc. Finally rinse thoroughly in clean water and after re-assembly hang the equipment up to dry.

Muslins
Great care must be taken when sterilizing muslin cloths used for cheese-making. These can be sterilized in the preparatory hypochlorite solution but great care has to be taken to rinse very thoroughly as any solution left in the cloth can have an inhibiting effect on the bacteria needed to help with the process of making the cheese. Because of this I prefer to boil these cloths thoroughly to sterilize them. You should dry them in sunlight.

Milk Stone
This is a white deposit which builds up on dairy utensils, especially in hard water areas. It is harmless but does provide another site for bacteria to harbour and so should be removed periodically. Sometimes the build-up can be prevented by the use of a different dairy detergent as different types react according to the type of water supply.

Metal Equipment

The milk stone can be removed with proprietary removers or phosphoric acid. Wire wool should never be used as this makes scratches in which bacteria can lurk. First wash the utensils in hot detergent-sterilizer then rinse in cold water. Always wear rubber gloves for this operation. If you are using a proprietary remover, follow the directions exactly. If using syrupy phosphoric acid (specific gravity 1.75) add, with great care, 90ml of acid to each 5 litres warm water in a plastic bucket (or plastic barrel if doing a quantity). Use this solution to brush all surfaces. After 5 minutes contact remove the loosened scale with a nylon scourer. Leave a while longer and repeat this procedure if the scale persists. Then rinse thoroughly and scrub in hot detergent-sterilizer to remove residual scale, acid and bacteria, giving a final rinse in clean cold water.

The undiluted acid must not be allowed to come into contact with skin, clothing or metal and must be kept out of the reach of children, and stock.

Rubber Components

The teat cup liners are liable to absorb fat from milk. For this reason synthetic components are better than rubber as they do not absorb fat in the same way. To remove the fat a long caustic soda soak is necessary. Really this means having two sets of rubbers. While one set is soaking for six days in a strong solution, either a preparatory one or five per cent caustic soda at 0.5kg per 10 litres of water, the other can be in use. The solution should be made up in a plastic container with a lid. Remember to add the caustic soda to the water; the other way is dangerous because of heat and effervescence. Wear rubber gloves and allow no contact with the skin. After the long soak the rubbers should be brushed in hot dairy detergent-sterilizer, rinsed and allowed to dry before finally re-assembling. The caustic soda solution should be renewed once a month. Remember, synthetic rubbers do *not* need this treatment which would only harden them. Be very careful when handling the acid, do not splash it, and, if you do, wash it off immediately under running water. Keep the container covered at all times and keep the acid out of the reach of children and stock.

The Dairy

The traditional farmhouse dairy is a thing of great beauty and interest. There are just a few of them left in England and Wales and more on the continent, where the *fermier* or farmhouse-scale dairy industry has not lost ground as it has done in the British Isles. If you get the chance to visit one and see it working it is very worthwhile. There are now several enterprising farm museums (see *Useful Addresses*) where an attempt has been made to create the pre-industrial revolution atmosphere in giving dairying demonstrations. This is picturesque and romantic but when one thinks of the real problems the dairymaid encountered prior to all the scientific developments e.g. pasteurization and refrigeration, I do not think one would wish to put the clock back. In many ways we now have the best of both worlds; we have an understanding of the basic scientific factors which will help us to produce the best dairy foods possible while, at the same time, putting the right value on the small-scale, more individual production methods.

In your own dairy, whether it is a fully equipped room or just a corner of your kitchen, you can produce dairy food which is absolutely yours, it will reflect your pasture, your particular animal, your taste and the taste of your family. This seems to me to be the most important motivating force for undertaking home dairying. It seems to me a far greater achievement to produce your very own farmhouse cheese, than to try to reproduce the great cheeses of the world. So my aim throughout is to encourage you to experiment, to make the most of your resources so that you can produce food that you and your family enjoy rather than any absolutely standard product.

The Perfect Location
If you have a building you can adapt as a dairy, it is worth doing. If not of course you can manage with a corner of the kitchen but as you become more skilful and keen you will find it frustrating to have to pack away all the equipment every time. Also, bearing in mind that bacteria begin to invade the milk the second it leaves the cow, the actual standard of physical cleanliness you need for dairy work is difficult to achieve in a kitchen which is used for many purposes, especially if it is the friendly country kitchen which is the heart of the house.

Ideally you need somewhere which can be kept dust and dirt free. A concrete or tiled floor which has a drain so that it can be hosed down, finely rendered concrete walls, (traditionally whitewashed with lime 'set' with skimmed milk) painted with washable paint, windows fitted

26 MAKING CHEESES, BUTTERS, CREAM AND YOGURT

with mesh if possible, to keep out flies, working surfaces of slate or marble and slatted draining boards through which the water drips directly on the floor. Hot and cold water should be laid on in a big sink, set down to facilitate the lifting in of large pans. The room should be north facing and the site well away from any contaminating sources such as dusty fodder stores, oil vapours or muck heaps.

Ventilation is important, as no drying up cloth should ever be used in a dairy. Air should be able to circulate but, and this is very important if the dairy is to be used as a cheese-making room there must be the possibility of bringing the temperature up to some 65°-70°F (18°-20°C) because in cheese-making it is important that the ambient temperature is high enough for the whey to drain from the curd. This is one of the most common misunderstandings and probably the reason so many efforts fail. The room must therefore be warm for cheese-making but milk, cream and butter must be kept cool. A refrigerator for the latter purpose and some sort of (safe) heater (traditionally in the larger dairies, hot pipes) for the former are necessary. If you are using your kitchen, you do score here on heating costs.

If you have a proper dairy keep nothing in it which is not absolutely required there. It should be bare and uncluttered and when you come into it you should put on a clean white coat or overall and clean (or at least well washed) boots.

Equipment

This is a brief list; further details will be given in the relevant sections.

General
- Electricity
- Water (hot and cold)
- A low sink
- A fridge for storing the milk

For Cream and Butter-making
- Cream setting pans, skimmer
- Clotted cream pans
- A butter churn
- A butter worker or wooden board
- Scotch hands
- A dairy thermometer
- A room thermometer

For Cheese-making
The big jacketed vats are hardly necessary for a home dairy but something which acts as a water bath is essential. This can be a large double saucepan, a large sized porringer or, for greater quantities, a Burco boiler and a churn. The milk in the churn can be heated by raising the temperature of the water in the boiler, and cooled by removing the churn from the boiler and inserting an in-churn cooler, which runs cold water through it. This is the best method for making cheeses with larger quantities of milk. You can of course improvise by running hot water into the sink and standing the pan of milk in it to heat, and then draining the sink and refilling it with cold water to cool the milk.

   Cheese press
   Chessit and follower
   Cheese moulds
   Straw or plastic mats and
   Cheese cloths
   An acidimeter
   Curd knives
   A variety of ladles, knives and measuring jugs.

Old books list many more items: curd rakes and scoops, wire curd breakers (these looked like square tennis racquets) as well as many types of tubs and moulds. Of course it is of interest to see and handle these things but they have become obsolete now because they are in the main, too small for mass production and too large for home use.

2

MILK RECIPES

DRINKS
Cooled, fresh milk is a delicious and nutritious drink on its own. Of course some people prefer it fresh from the cow at blood heat.

Milk Shakes
These can be made easily by combining milk with home-made concentrated fruit syrup and adding a portion of home made ice-cream (see below). Such a home-made milk shake will put to shame the most expensive, bought concoctions.

Milk can be heated to make cocoa, hot chocolate and malted milk all soothing bed-time drinks for which no instructions are necessary. As alternatives try:

Treacle Milk
Heat 1 pint (550ml) of milk, add 2 teaspoonsful of black treacle, float a little cream on the top and dust with cinnamon powder.

Mexican Chocolate
Make up drinking chocolate and add one part of strong black coffee to every two parts of drinking chocolate. Add a few drops of vanilla essence or some vanilla sugar and plenty of whipped cream. Can be hot or iced. Vanilla sugar is castor sugar in which a couple of vanilla pods have been kept. Its subtle flavour goes excellently with milk.

Egg Flip
Beat an egg with a tablespoonful of castor or brown sugar, add a measure of sherry and $\frac{1}{2}$ pint (275ml) hot (not boiled) milk. Heat gently stirring all the time but do not boil.

Lait du Poule
This is a West Indian pick-me-up, said to be good for colds and sore throats.
 Beat an egg yolk with a tot of rum. Heat $\frac{1}{2}$ pint (275ml) of milk and

add 1 tablespoonful of honey. Pour this onto the egg and rum and drink at once.

Party Egg Nog *(for large numbers)*
12 eggs
10 oz. (275g) castor sugar
1 pint (550ml) milk
1 pint (550ml) rum, cognac or sherry
1 pint (550ml) cream
Cinnamon or nutmeg.

Beat egg yolks and sugar until they form a perfectly smooth cream which will fall from the beater in a 'ribbon'. Add milk and alcohol little by little. Put in fridge for 2 hours to take off 'eggy' taste. At last minute whip egg whites into a foam and float on bowl then top with cream.

Old-fashioned Drinks
As well as these well known drinks there exist a host of less known ones which were popular with our ancestors. These are the caudels and possetts which have become almost extinct over the last century, but which might give us pleasure to sample again. Before refrigeration milk was encouraged to curdle, partly because this was inevitable and partly because it was (rightly) believed that the curd was easy to digest and good for one.

> 'A sparing diet did her health assure
> Or, sick, a possett was her cure.'
>
> Dryden

A Simple Possett
Heat 1 pint (550ml) of milk in a pan until it froths up, add a measure of white wine. Strain out the curd, rub in some sugar and a squeeze of lemon and finish with a grate of nutmeg.

Possetts were not only used medicinally but taken in place of a meal. In the days of long journeys which could not be interrupted for a proper meal a possett was taken to 'be going on with'. They were usually served in china possett dishes.

Pope's Possett

'From far Barbados on the Western main
Fetch sugar ounces four, fetch sac from Spain
One pint, and from the Eastern coast
Nutmeg: the glory of the Northern toast,
On Flaming coals let them together heat
Till the all conquering sac dissolves the sweet.
On such another fire put eggs, just ten
(New-born from tread of cock and rump of hen)
Stir them with steady hand, and conscience pricking
To see the untimely end of ten fine chicken.
From shining shelf, take down the brazen skillet
A quart of milk from gentle cow will fill it,
When boiled and cold, put milk to sac and eggs
Unite them firmly, like the triple league
And on the fire let them together dwell.'

Milk Punch (This is another old recipe taken from *Glasse*, 1742)
'Beat 15 eggs well and strain onto $\frac{3}{4}$ lb white sugar and 1 pint canary wine. Set over coals until it is scalding hot. Grate some nutmeg into a quart of milk, boil it and pour it onto the scalding eggs and wine. Hold your hand high (or pour from off kitchen table) to froth up. Set before fire half an hour, then serve.'

Milk and Brandy Punch

Pour 1 pint (550ml) of milk into a pan add $\frac{1}{2}$ rind of lemon, 12 lumps of sugar and simmer for 15 minutes. Remove rind and add a beaten egg and a measure of brandy.

A Simple Caudel

Caudels served a similar purpose to possetts in that they were taken to stave off hunger during journeys, they were generally more substantial than the possett, a sort of 'soup wine' or 'ale meal' with gruel or oatmeal in them.

Take 1 tablespoonful of oatmeal and add 1 cupful of cold water. Pour on one pint (550ml) of milk, boil for 4-5 minutes, stirring continuously. Add 1 egg yolk and a glass of sherry or port, 3 lumps of sugar and a grating of lemon rind or nutmeg.

Wine Whey

Curds and whey were separated in many ways, flavoured and then served together but as separate entities.

Wine Whey is made by boiling a cupful of milk and then adding to it a small glass of wine or sherry. This is stirred and left until the curds and whey separate, then strained and a little sugar added to sweeten the whey with a grating of nutmeg sprinkled over the curd. The whey was either served in a jug or poured back over the curd.

London Syllabub
Syllabubs have made a come-back recently and feature on the menus of quite a number of restaurants. They are usually made with cream (see also p55) nowadays. *Sille* is derived from the name of a district in the Champagne area of France, and the word *bub*, an Elizabethan term for anything frothy.

Put $1\frac{1}{2}$ pints (825ml) white wine in a bowl and add sugar to taste. Pour on 2 quarts of fresh milk and grate a little nutmeg over. Cover thickly with clotted cream and dust the top with fine sugar and a sprinkling of cinnamon.

All these dishes with milk, alcohol, nutmeg and cinnamon, have a certain flavour of the past, a flavour that is echoed today only in the nutmeg which we commonly enjoy on rice pudding. Many of the spice flavours came to us from the Middle East at the time of the crusades and much cookery in Morocco today is similar to that in England at that time. One of the most basic of medieval flavours was that of the almond, still widely used in Eastern cookery.

Milk of Almonds
This features so much in early English cookery and seems to have been a sort of syrup which was used extensively for flavouring. In France orgeat, or barley water, was flavoured with almonds and produced a similar syrup or 'milk'.

To make a modern equivalent, simmer 2 oz. (50g) coarsely ground almonds (with a few bitter ones) with $\frac{1}{2}$ cupful of milk for 10 minutes. This can be added to milk puddings etc.

A more authentic version of this syrup is given in Claudia Roden's superb book *A Book of Middle Eastern Food* (see *Suggested Further Reading*) in which the 'milk' is simply the milk liquid exuded by the almonds. A syrup of this is obtained by tying $\frac{1}{2}$ lb (225g) ground almonds in a muslin bag and soaking them in $1\frac{1}{2}$ pints (825ml) of water until the almond 'milk' has come out. The almond water is then boiled with at least 2 lbs (900g) sugar to make a long lasting syrup which will coat the back of a spoon. Just as the pan is removed from the heat the syrup is perfumed with 2 tablespoonsful of orange blossom water. This syrup is delicious diluted with ice-cold water as a drink.

Junket

While the last item has little to do with real milk, junket is quite the opposite. Traditionally it was made with milk warm from the cow; some even say the milk was milked straight into the junket dish. It is one of the few milky dishes which has never been right out of fashion, probably because it is so simple.

1 pint (550ml) of milk, 2 level tablespoonsful of sugar, 1 dessertspoonful of junket rennet (this is weaker than cheese-making rennet) or the appropriate number of junket rennet tablets. The sugar can be vanilla sugar (i.e. castor sugar in which a vanilla pod has been kept) or a few drops of pure vanilla essence may be added. Put the pan of milk on the stove and heat to blood heat (unless milk is straight from cow) add the sugar and rennet, stirring well. If you wish to flavour differently blend some flavouring with a little of the milk and mix this back with the rest. Put in the bowls in which it is to be served and leave to set. Purists claim that a junket's flavour is lost if it is refrigerated but modern taste prefers cold dishes very cold. Dorothy Hartley in her magnificent book *Food in England* (see *Suggested Further Reading*) mentions that creams, blancmanges and jellies were traditionally set 'stone cold' i.e. being kept on the stone floors of the underground cellars at the lowest temperatures possible prior to refrigeration: milk dishes and junkets were served dairy cold, and custards usually just cold. The distinctions were subtle and freezing could destroy aromas.

Junkets were often flavoured with rum and served with a cap of cream.

Koumiss

The normal fermentation of milk by lactic acid can be followed by an alcoholic fermentation if yeasts gain access to the milk, as yeasts are not inhibited by acidity. Yeasts are classed as contaminants if they get into milk accidentally but use is made of this fact in the preparation of some Middle Eastern drinks.

Koumiss is made by dissolving $\frac{1}{4}$ oz. (6g) yeast in 2 tablespoonsful of warm water and adding this with 2 tablespoonsful of sugar to a quart (about 1 litre) of warm milk. Pour into airtight bottles leaving 1½ inches at the top. Invert and leave for 6 hours at a warm temperature 80°F (27°C). Serve next day well chilled.

Kéfir
Kéfir is a more elaborate form of koumiss. The kéfir grains, which contain yeast and a culture can be obtained from Chris Hansen Laboratories (see *Useful Addresses*). They look something like florets of cauliflower and must be soaked for 2 hours in tepid water before being put in milk which has been boiled and then cooled to 71°F (22°C) at the rate of a dessertspoonful per pint. An equal quantity of sugar should be added and the vessel covered and left for 24 hours. The next day strain into screw-top bottles which should not be quite full. They will be ready in 2-3 days and contain a pleasant fizzy drink. The grains can be washed, dried and used again; however, they must be washed every two days to keep them alive. They are a strain of lactic acid bacteria which becomes gelatinous on contact with milk.

Salep
This is another Middle Eastern drink which you might like to try. It is made from milk and resin which can be found now in many Middle Eastern grocery shops either in powdered or, more rarely, in solid form (in which case of course it will need pulverizing).

For 1 pint (550ml) of milk take 1 teaspoonful of salep powder and heat the milk adding the salep and stirring all the time until it thickens. Serve sprinkled with finely ground pistachio nuts and cinnamon.

This is known as salepi in Greece and the resin gives it a strange, characteristic flavour.

MILK PUDDINGS
Milk puddings have rather a 'school dinner' reputation, which is a pity because they can be so delicious. If you have your own cow or goat and can make them with rich creamy milk you will be pleasantly surprised with even such nursery stand-bys as rice pudding.

Rice Pudding
To cook any of the cereal based milk puddings you need a slow oven – the Aga or Rayburn type are excellent.

There are two main methods:

1. Butter the dish and cover with $\frac{1}{4}$ inch of rice, cover this with 3-4 inches fresh creamy milk and a level tablespoonful of vanilla sugar. (You can use ordinary sugar and vanilla essence but by now you will be aware that I prefer to use vanilla sugar. It combines very well with milk and the vanilla pod can be washed and used again and again.) Cover closely and bake, stirring from time to time at first until the rice is swollen, then uncover and cook for a further 3-4 hours.
2. Bring the milk and sugar to the boil while you butter the dish, then place in the oven for four hours. Finish with a grate of nutmeg.

Basic Proportions for Milk Puddings
Powdered grains (ground rice, semolina etc.) 1-1$\frac{1}{2}$ oz. per pint of milk. Whole grains (rice, barley, sago, tapioca) 1$\frac{1}{2}$ oz. (40g) per pint. Flaked cereals (oats, barley, flaked rice) 1$\frac{1}{2}$-2 oz. (40-50g) per pint.

Flavourings
These are a matter of personal taste but vanilla, nutmeg and cinnamon are traditionally good. Currants, dates, raisins and chocolate can also be used.

Similarly there are two basic methods
1. Grease pie dish, pour in milk, washed grains and sugar (and flavourings). Allow to stand for an hour or so. Cook slowly until creamy; finish with a grating or topping of something suitable.
2. Rinse a saucepan with water to prevent scorching. Put milk and washed grains in and cook until tender, stirring vigorously. Add sugar and flavouring and pour into buttered dish to finish in the oven.

Fluffin
Cover some barley in a pan and simmer until very smooth, stirring all the time. Just before serving add sugar, nutmeg and, if liked, a little brandy. Serve with thick cream.

Frumenty
Simmer kibbled wheat in milk in a low oven overnight or for 12 hours. Add mixed spices, currants and a little rum. Once again serve with thick cream. A traditional north country farmhouse dish, served at Christmas time.

MILK RECIPES

Hasties

This is an old farmhouse stand-by for the house with, 'Some flour in the bin, a cow in the byre and some butter in the crock' (1742). It is one of many batter based recipes.

Break an egg into flour and work to a stiff paste. Add boiling milk, some sugar, a little salt and a spoonful of orange or rose water and some butter, keep stirring until thick and smooth, pour it out and butter the top adding cinnamon and brown sugar.

Many improvized dishes can be made with batter. Dorothy Hartley gives a fruit batter made by the fruit pickers in the vale of Evesham. This is tasty, quick and suitable for almost any fruit available. Put a handful of fruit in the oven in a pot with sugar. Then make a batter with flour, egg, milk and cook this in individual saucer shaped patty pans. When these are cooked lift out one batter, fill with fruit and cover with another. A few peas or green beans can be used instead of fruit, in which case the batter is flavoured with salt and pepper. I have some patty pans which make batters just the right size to contain a lightly poached egg or an *oeuf en cocotte*. This makes a change from poached egg on toast.

Soyer's Bread and Milk

Alexis Soyer, the great chef who cooked for kings and beggars, invented a marvellous stove and was a great creative chef. He also had a lot of time for the simple things and the following is an example:

> 'Boil 1 pint (550ml) of milk with $\frac{1}{4}$ oz. (6g) sugar, cut the crusts into small pieces and put in a hot bowl. Put 2 small pieces of butter onto the crusts, a grate of nutmeg and a pinch of cinnamon. Pour the boiling milk over and cover closely. Keep hot for 5 minutes and eat at once without stirring or spoiling the texture.'

This is a good way of using crusts removed for other dishes. Brown bread and milk with lots of soft brown sugar, warm but not boiled milk and a topping of cream is delicious too – a quick and enjoyable food for children.

Custards

Custards too have a rather poor image and yet can be the most delicious of puddings. Much confusion arises over the name alone; there is the ubiquitous yellow shop-bought powdered 'custard', invented over 100 years ago by the Birmingham grocer Alfred Bird; there is also real or 'egg' custard made by boiling milk and sweetening it and flavouring it with vanilla and beating into it eggs (or egg yolks) until the preparation thickens. This is now a custard sauce, (known to the French as an *anglaise*) or what the old recipes call a 'cream'. If put in a dish in the oven in a bain-marie this becomes a baked custard. The secret here once again is slow cooking to create a really creamy pudding. The creamier the milk the more delicious the results, so this section overlaps to some extent with that on cooking with cream (see page 56).

There are innumerable variations on the theme of the custard but it should always have a subtle delicate flavour. Here is an old recipe.

'Take a quantity of milk and set it to boil in a heavy pan ... while it is boiling cut thick snippetts of bread and lay them in a dish. Have ready six egg yolks strained with rosewater and syrup. Take the milk off the fire, stir in the egg and pour onto the bread. Leave to be cold.'

Crème Caramel

Prepare the caramel by heating 6 tablespoonsful of castor sugar, stirring until it melts and adding a squeeze of lemon juice. Stir over heat until this darkens but do not let it burn for this makes it bitter. Add a little water as it bubbles. Pour this liquid into individual moulds swishing it around to coat the sides.

Make a custard, scald 1 pint (550ml) of milk with 2 oz. (50g) sugar (vanilla). Beat 4 eggs and gradually add cooled milk to them. Stir the custard well and pour into the moulds. Place them in a dish of water and cover with tinfoil or greaseproof paper and bake in a moderate oven until set. Allow to cool and turn out. The creamier the milk the better the crème.

Crème Patissière

This is the French counterpart of the English custard; it is used in pastries and is the one notable exception to the rule than one should not boil a preparation containing eggs.

Boil 1 pint (550ml) of milk with a vanilla pod, mix $\frac{1}{4}$ lb (100g) flour $\frac{1}{2}$ lb (225g) sugar and add 5 beaten egg yolks and 2 whole eggs. Pour the hot milk onto this mixture and boil it up stirring all the time until the consistency of mayonnaise is attained. Remove the vanilla pod and cool.

This is the basis for *Petits Pots de Crème*, small individual deep pots filled with vanilla, chocolate, strawberry, raspberry or banana flavoured crème patissière.

Blancmange or Shape
This is now a rather unfashionable pudding but children still enjoy it, especially if a decorative mould can be found. In Edwardian days a plain white shape, turned onto a white dish and carefully garnished with, perhaps, a scarlet geranium or some maidenhair fern, was greatly appreciated.

From one pint (550ml) of milk take enough to blend $1\frac{1}{2}$ oz. (50g) of cornflour with 2 oz. (50g) castor sugar and a pinch of salt. Blend to a paste. Bring remaining milk to boil and stir it slowly into the cornflour mixture. Return all to the heat and bring back to the boil and simmer stirring for about ten minutes. Pour into a well moistened mould and set.

As with all milk based dishes, delicate flavourings are best: lemon, almond, coffee etc. They should be mixed with the original blending milk.

Treacle Blancmange
This is made by stirring 2 tablespoonsful of treacle into the cornflour and blending milk instead of sugar. A melted syrup sauce may be poured over the blancmange as it is served.

Beestings or Calf's Milk
Beestings or beistyn is the colostrum which the cow yields for a few days immediately after calving. On no account should the calf be denied this important food as it clears his digestive tract and is full of essential vitamins to help him combat infection.

Many cows however give more than the calf can take and although it is illegal to sell it, there has always been a country tradition that a jug of it should be given to friends, and that the jug should not come back empty (or it would bode ill for the calf!).

It is a thick yellow creamy substance with the consistency of egg yolk and makes lovely custards or cakes.

Calf's Milk Custard
One cupful of milk to 2-3 cupsful of beestings. Add $\frac{1}{2}$ cupful of sugar

and stir in double boiler over gentle heat until dissolved. Then cook slowly for about 2 hours.

Beestings Cake
A traditional type of custard tart. The above custard is turned into pastry tarts or tartlets and these are baked. They are eaten cold.

3
YOGURT

Yogurt is a cultured milk i.e. one which has been treated by heat to destroy rival bacteria and into which the required bacteria have subsequently been introduced and given the most favourable conditions to multiply.

It is a method of preserving milk for a little longer than it would last as whole milk and has a very long history, going back to the Bible. It has always been used extensively in the Middle East and Greece and has had many therapeutic qualities attributed to it, including those connected with longevity.

Yogurt came to Europe at around the beginning of the sixteenth century when King François I of France was taken ill and a doctor summoned from Constantinople. He arrived some time later with a herd of sheep and goats from the milk of which he made yogurt and gave the French king a bowl a day. The king recovered and asked for the recipe but the doctor would not reveal the secret and returned with his goats and sheep to Constantinople. The French were so impressed that they thought it a miracle and they named yogurt *le lait de la vie éternelle*.

This theory that yogurt prolonged life and enhanced virility was investigated in 1908 by the scientist and Nobel Prize winner Metchnikoff who studied at the Pasteur Institute. His studies isolated the yogurt bacteria which made possible the production of yogurt on a commercial scale. It was never actually proved that yogurt had any influence on longevity but *lactobacillus bulgaricus*, the most common yogurt bacteria, was named after the race who hold the record for long lives.

There are still many strange theories about yogurt today. At first it was thought that colonies of *l. bulgaricus* would become established in the intestines of regular yogurt eaters and would aid digestion. Now this is no longer believed to be the case; these bacteria cannot establish themselves within the human body. There are two other bacteria however, *l. acidophilus* and *l. bifidis*, which have been found to establish themselves in the human intestines and yogurt freaks are adamant that they break down food as it digests, curtail the growth of putrefactive bacteria and aid the synthesis of vitamins B and K. They especially recommend the ingestion of these bacteria after courses of penicillin or other such drugs which do kill off the good bacteria with the bad. The traditional starters can be obtained either by buying some live yogurt, borrowing some from a friend who has a good culture going, or sending off to a stockist for a 'starter'. These can be obtained from Chris Hansen Laboratories and other stockists (see *Useful Addresses*). Hansen's also stock *l. acidophilus* which also retails under the name of 'Enpac' and can be obtained from Aplin and Barrett of Yeovil in Somerset.

Making Yogurt
Making yogurt is so simple; there is no mystique about it at all. There are many methods and first I will describe how I make it, every four or five days.

Take 2 pints (about 1 litre) of milk and bring to a rolling boil. Remove from heat until you can put your finger in (110°F, 43°C) and count ten. Put a teaspoonful of yogurt (bought, borrowed or culture) into a dish and pour on the milk, stirring to mix culture in thoroughly. Cover with a clean table napkin and leave in a warm place (not the top of the fridge) overnight. In the morning it will have become thick creamy yogurt and should be put in the fridge.

Alternative Methods
Most alternative methods are employed when there is no constant heat source such as the back of the stove or an airing cupboard which maintains the sort of heat which the yogurt needs to incubate successfully.
1. Wide necked thermos flask. The yogurt will incubate successfully but may break up a little when getting it out.
2. A bought or home-made incubating box. There are quite a number of yogurt-making kits available which work very well. You can however, construct yourself a small incubating box which will not only serve as a yogurt-maker but also come in very handy for incubating your cheese starter. It consists simply of a wooden box, with a close fitting lid, well insulated (for example, with polystyrene ceiling tiles) and fitted with an electric bulb. The temperature inside the box can be regulated by the

YOGURT

strength of bulb used. The size of the box can depend on size and type of container which you wish to put in it.

3. A Haybox. This works in exactly the same way as the incubating box.
4. The oven turned off. If you have finished cooking, you can make use of the heat which is left in the oven for yogurt making.
5. An electric pad or blanket turned very low.
6. Putting the yogurt in the sun. If you make yogurt in a clear pyrex dish and place it in the sun, and ensure that it does not become shaded, it is possible to maintain an adequate temperature.
7. In a baby's bottle warmer set low. This is a good way to make small amounts and would suit someone living alone.

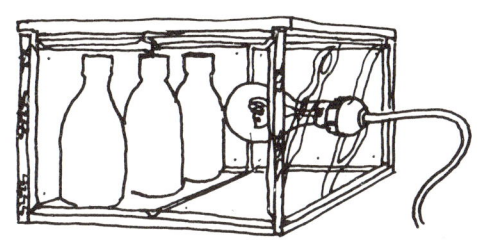

Figure 5. Incubating box for yogurt or cheese starter

The yogurt can of course be made in one large dish or in individual pots. If you are making the latter, mix milk and culture very thoroughly to ensure that each pot gets some starter, or put a small quantity in each pot and stir the milk in thoroughly.

Possible Errors

If your mixture does not 'yog' the fault may be due to one of the following:

1. Perhaps you forgot the starter completely.
2. Maybe you added it at the wrong temperature. If too hot the milk can kill it, if too cold it will not grow.
3. Perhaps the culture was too weak, although the use of more starter because you fear it is weak does not always work. About every month or so it is a good idea to renew your starter although theoretically there is no need to do so and of course the Middle Eastern nomads who eat so much yogurt never do.

4. Maybe something else has killed off the culture—antibiotics in the milk or sterilizing solution inadequately rinsed from utensils.

Texture and Flavour
Yogurt varies a lot in texture and flavour. Yogurt can be made thin by whipping it up. It can be thickened by adding powdered milk (about 25 per cent more) to liquid milk or by making with powdered milk and 25 per cent less water. The curd can be contracted by heating, prior to draining it.

The flavour of yogurt can vary from mild to very acid indeed. The milk yogurt sold in Europe in the supermarkets would scarcely be recognizable as such to the tribesmen of the Middle East. If you want a mild yogurt you should chill it just as it begins to set. The longer the yogurt is left to incubate, the more acid it becomes.

Yogurt can be made from any milk and is made from cow's, goat's, ewe's, asses', mare's and buffalo's milk in different parts of the world. It can also be made from any type of milk: raw, pasteurized, skimmed, or any sort of powdered milk (reconstituted with water of course).

Commercially yogurt-making is a huge worldwide industry and every flavour and type, ranging from champagne rhubarb yogurt to yogurt-on-a-stick, is now marketed.

YOGURT RECIPES
In Europe yogurt is thought of mainly as a dessert food. It has found great favour amongst slimmers as an alternative to cream as it is quite low in calories. Almost any type of fruit or flavouring can be added to yogurt but with home-made yogurt my personal preference is for plain yogurt eaten *with* variously flavoured foods. Here are some examples: plain yogurt with honey and a dusting of wheatgerm or nuts; plain yogurt with home-made crab-apple jam; plain yogurt with well sweetened prunes, or, better still, with very syrupy prune juice.

Also, any home-made jams which do not set properly can become excellent sauces to go with yogurt.

Flavouring Yogurt
Although I like plain yogurt, many people prefer it flavoured. There are two different methods of introducing the flavouring agent: by infusion and by blending. If flavouring agents are added prior to incubation, they can inhibit the yogurt-making bacteria, so it is necessary to add

them after the yogurt has thickened. In doing so of course the yogurt becomes broken but will usually firm up again if allowed to stand for a while.

Infusion
This method works well, a solid and highly flavoured ingredient is put into the yogurt and removed prior to eating. If part of the item is left sticking out it can usually be pulled out without breaking the yogurt too much. Possible flavourers include: a vanilla pod; a spring onion; a cinnamon stick; any herbs; or a piece of peeled garlic on a stick.

Mixing or Blending
Here are some suggestions for mixing or blending flavourings: vanilla essence; flower water; honey or maple syrup; or chocolate or cocoa powder. Solid flavourings, like dried fruit or desiccated coconut, can be added if finely chopped. Fruit and nuts can be used but should only be added immediately before eating.

Although in Europe yogurt is thought of mainly as a sweet or dessert item, in the Middle East it has accompanied the savoury course, as well as being used in cooking and in making a very refreshing drink.

Laban
This cooling drink is made simply by combining equal quantities of yogurt and water in a blender with a good bunch of fresh mint and a little salt. Serve chilled with a lump of ice.

Cakik or Cucumber Salad
Yogurt is delicious in salads and this is my favourite.
One small cucumber
2-3 cloves of garlic
½ pint (275ml) yogurt
3 tablespoonsful of fresh chopped mint

Dice the cucumber and sprinkle liberally with salt in a colander, leave to drain for an hour – a lot of liquid will come out. Crush the garlic and mix into the yogurt and when adequately drained, add the cucumber. At the last moment add the mint. Tomatoes can be added too, if liked. Serve with pitta bread.

Cooking with Yogurt

Yogurt may be added to soups, stews etc. in much the same way as cream. In order to prevent curdling however, it must be added at the end of the cooking process. If you wish to cook the yogurt, it must first be 'stabilized' to prevent the curdling. There are two ways of doing this using either cornflour or egg whites.

Beat the yogurt in a large saucepan until liquid, add egg white or cornflour (1 egg white or 1 tablespoonful of cornflour to 2 pints (about 1 litre) of yogurt) mixed to a paste with a little water. Bring to the boil stirring constantly with a wooden spoon *in one direction only* then turn heat as low as possible for about ten minutes. Do not cover, as drops of liquid would spoil it.

This stabilized yogurt will keep for a much longer time and can be used in all sorts of ways in cookery. Many Middle Eastern dishes call for it. Claudia Roden in her *A Book of Middle Eastern Food* suggests this following idea.

Immos

This means literally 'lamb in his mother's milk'.

2 lbs (900g) lamb cut in cubes
2 medium onions
Salt and black pepper
1 pint (550ml) yogurt
2 cloves garlic, crushed
1 teaspoonful of ground coriander
2 tablespoonsful of butter

Steam the meat with onions for about $1\frac{1}{2}$ hours. (This can be pressure cooked.) Salt and pepper to taste. It must be extremely soft and tender. Stabilize the yogurt and add to cooked meat and simmer for 15 minutes. Fry the crushed garlic and coriander in butter and pour over the meat. Serve with saffron rice.

Chenna and Panir

In Indian cookery there are similar uses of yogurt. *Dahi* is a form of Indian yogurt. Normally made with buffalo milk which is extremely rich, it does not taste quite the same here but yogurt made with really creamy Channel Island milk can be a substitute.

Heat $1\frac{1}{2}$ pints (825ml) milk stirring continuously to prevent skin forming. When it comes to the boil remove from the heat and add $\frac{1}{4}$ teaspoonful of tartaric acid ($\frac{1}{2}$ squeezed lemon or $\frac{1}{2}$ squeezed lime used as a substitute) dissolved in either hot water or whey. Stir gently until the whole curdles. Leave covered for 15 minutes, strain through a muslin. The curds thus formed are chenna and are often used in Indian sweets.

Panir is the same thing but pressed into cubes. These often accompany curries. There is a section on this in Mrs Balbir Singh's *Indian Cookery* (see *Suggested Further Reading*).

Ukrainian Kasha
Yogurt combines well with cereals as this recipe shows.
4 oz. (100g) of buckwheat groats (kasha)
¾ pint (425ml) of scalded milk
2 oz. (50g) cottage cheese
4 oz. (100g) yogurt
2 eggs

Roast the grains until they are brown. Mix with the milk, cheese yogurt and beaten eggs. Season with salt and pepper. Spoon this onto a baking dish and cook for 40 minutes in a moderate oven.

Yogurt is very good with baked fish too; pour over at the end of cooking and lay slices of lemon on top. Yogurt can also be used in baking, here is a recipe for a traditional Balkan or Middle Eastern cake.

Balkan Yogurt Cake
6 oz. (175g) butter
6 oz. (175g) sugar
2 eggs
8 oz. (225g) yogurt
8 oz. (225g) flour
2 teaspoonsful of baking powder
½ teaspoonful of bicarbonate of soda
½ teaspoonful of salt
2 teaspoonsful of finely grated lemon rind
Icing sugar

Cream butter and sugar and add eggs one at a time, stir in the lemon rind and yogurt. Sift flour, baking powder and bicarbonate of soda and salt. Beat until smooth.

Turn into greased dish and bake at 350°F (177°C, gas mark 4) until cooked (about 35 minutes). Cool for 5 minutes, then turn onto rack. Dredge liberally with icing sugar and eat while warm.

Yogurt Cheese
Yogurt cheese can be made by draining the whey out of yogurt. To do so place two or three layers of muslin over a colander and pour the yogurt into it. Leave to drain for two or three hours and then suspend the cloth so that more whey comes out.

It is best if the yogurt used has already thickened a good deal and as yogurt gets more tart as it ages, this cheese, known as Lebanie, is fairly strong tasting.

In the Middle East it is served with olive oil and olives and pitta bread which compliment its piquant flavour.

4

CREAM

Milk fat, the constituent of cream, exists in minute globules, 0.001-0.0001mm in size, suspended in the milk serum. The specific gravity of the serum is 1.036 and that of the fat 0.95 so the fat globules obviously rise to the top and form a creamy layer.

This layer, in which some casein is enmeshed, is particularly rich in vitamin A and is classed as different types of cream according to how much fat it contains. Here is a list of these different types of cream.

1. *Clotted cream.* This contains at least 55 per cent butterfat and is a 'manufactured' cream made by a traditional method which gives it its characteristic flavour (see below).
2. *Double cream.* This contains at least 48 per cent butterfat and is a rich pouring cream. There is also a homogenized double cream which will not keep.
3. *Whipping cream.* This contains 35 per cent butterfat, this being the ideal butterfat content for a good whipping cream. This cream will double its volume when whipped.
4. *Sterilized cream.* This contains 23 per cent butterfat and is treated with heat and canned for long life.
5. *Single cream.* This contains at least 18 per cent butterfat.
6. *Half cream* (top of the milk). This contains a minimum of 12 per cent butterfat.

Separation

Cream can be separated from cow's milk by several methods. The warmer the milk the quicker the cream will rise.

1. The milk can be put in a shallow vessel known as a cream-setting pan and the cream removed by skimming either with a saucer, or a proper 'fleeter' with holes in it. (A good substitute is a scallop shell, traditionally used in the West country clotted cream-making processes, the ridges drain the milk away.) Some are fitted with a lip to facilitate pouring off the milk.
2. A similar method is a setting device with a plug in it through which the milk can be drained off. This can either be in the form

of a shallow setting pan or a deep pan with a plug or a tap attached.
3. Another very satisfactory improvised device is the sweet jar method, where the milk is contained in a large glass jar which shows the cream line very clearly. A length of plastic tubing or a wine syphon can be inserted below the cream line and the milk syphoned off, leaving the cream in the jar. This is particularly useful if you are saving up cream for butter-making.

These methods of separation are perfectly adequate if you have plenty of milk from your cow and need the cream either for domestic butter-making, or for cooking with or for using as a garnish. They separate about 90 per cent of the cream and it has a butterfat content of about 50 per cent. They leave a milk quite acceptable for domestic use.

If however, you have a goat or you want to extract the maximum amount of cream from your milk because you want either to sell it, or to convert it into clotted cream, then you will need a cream separator.

Hand Operated Cream Separators.
These are on the market once again. Very good news for home dairy workers indeed. They can be obtained from Self Sufficiency and Smallholding Supplies (see *Useful Addresses*) who not only stock several sizes but also stock the parts with which the old hand separators (and there are still many about, some in perfect working order) can be mended.

Electric Cream Separators. These are very efficient indeed. Unfortunately this is reflected in their price.

A separator is a centrifugal device, which works sideways just as gravity works downwards. It spins the lighter cream towards the centre where it is drawn off by one pipe, while the heavier milk remains on the outside and is drawn off by another. This is a very efficient method as it removes almost all the cream and can be set to various 'thicknesses'. The only disadvantage is that the remaining milk is real 'skim' and, while very useful for cooking and feeding to stock (commercially it is dried or evaporated or condensed), it is not of good enough quality for domestic use as a 'drinking' milk.

If you use a separator the milk should be run through straight from the animal – if not it must be warmed to 104°F (40°C) for the best results. For goat milkers and those wishing to extract as much cream as possible from their cow's milk there is no substitute, but a separator has some 48 moveable parts which have to be cleaned thoroughly every time it is used and this can make the use of it troublesome unless it is really needed.

The density of the cream is adjusted by two factors, the pressure at which the milk is poured into the separator and the pressure of the cream screw. It is because of the latter that, if you are buying a second-hand separator, either see it working with the sort of milk you will be using, or have it on 'sale or return' so that you can try it out. Now that parts which fit the older models can be obtained the outlook is better, but until recently many old models on the market would not adjust properly and were very disappointing.

Pasteurization of Cream

If you wish to pasteurize your cream, here is how you do it. Pour the cream into a vessel and put this into a water bath containing hot water, put on the stove and raise the temperature of the cream to 145°F (63°C) and hold there for 30 minutes, stirring frequently. Cool at once to 40°F (14°C) by removing the vessel from the water bath and putting it into a sink, or container of running water.

How to Whip Cream

Cream whips much better if 'aged' a little. After pasteurization age for at least 24 hours at 40°F (14°C) to allow re-solidification of fatty elements. Even ageing bought cream gives better results. Make sure that all the equipment as well as the cream, are cool. Whip slowly at first then, as the cream becomes frothy, increase the speed. Do not overwhip or you will produce butter!

Clotted Cream

This is a speciality of Devon and Cornwall where a thriving postal trade still exists and where 'cream teas' are a part of the tourist trade.

It is made with the rich cow's milk of the south Devon cattle (although of course other breeds such as the Channel Island produce a milk rich enough for use for this purpose).

Clotted or 'clouted' is a word derived from 'clout', a thick piece of leather and implies that the cream can have changed very little over the years. Basically it is a scalded cream which develops a characteristic nutty, caramel flavour.

It was originally made in heavy earthenware pancheons over the gentle heat of peat fires. The steady heat of the heavy pans helped the procedure for not only did they warm very slowly but they also cooled slowly, which had a bearing on the final product. Traditionally clotted cream was made from the whole milk. The evenings milking or 'meal' was used as it is richer and the cream rises more easily.

There is now a commercial clotted cream trade and the scalding pans are manufactured for this purpose.

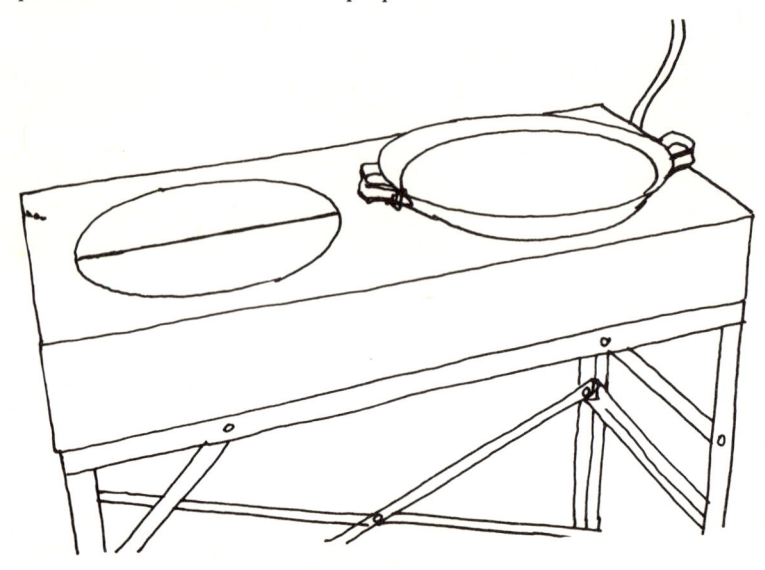

Figure 6. Scalding apparatus for clotted cream

If you wish to make clotted cream in quantity, use either a large preserving pan for the water and a large flat saucepan for the cream. Alternatively a frame can be fitted over an old copper, this is a satisfactory way of preventing the cream from scorching.

Method
Heat the milk in the jacketed apparatus to a temperature of 170°-190°F (77°-88°C) for about 40-50 minutes. Small bubbles will form beneath the cream level which should be wrinkled but not broken. Practice and eye are the only real guide as to when to remove the pan from the heat.

If the weather is cool the pan can be cooled on dairy shelves for 12-24 hours. If it is hot it is better cooled by circulating cold water around the jacketed apparatus, although air cooling however is said to produce the best flavour. For this reason cooling under refrigeration is not advocated as it causes a lot of flavour loss.

Skimming
If the cream is skimmed too soon a lot is lost in the milk. If left too long before skimming off-flavours can result, especially in warm weather. The cream should be removed from round the edges with a knife and then from off the top with a fleeter or skimmer (or a scallop shell) and the skim milk should be allowed to drain off thoroughly. The legal butterfat requirement for clotted cream being sold is 55 per cent, which is quite high so it is worth being careful over this.

The cream is then packed into tins, cartons or jars. An unbroken layer on the top gives a good finish. All this is very labour intensive which is one reason why it has stayed a relatively 'farmhouse' trade and is accordingly quite suitable for those involved in self-sufficiency who want to earn some extra money. As with all the dairying activities for sale to the public however, fairly stringent regulations are in force.

Faults
Great care must be taken throughout the operation not to let the cream acquire any external taints. The flavour is to some extent determined by the food the cow has eaten and this too can adversely affect the finished product (see p 18). The small amount of ripening during the setting period gives much of the characteristic flavour. It is quite illegal to add nisin or any other flavouring to cream being sold.

The flavour of clotted cream is very particular. Cream itself contains so many different elements which influence taste and texture. The olein in the fat gives the mellow taste and the stearin binds the whole together. In clotted cream it is a combination of the process, the ripeness and even the fact that the milk is whole rather than separated which go to make up this characteristic texture and taste.

Careless methods of milk production will of course result in contaminated cream with poor keeping qualities.
1. Streaky cream can result from overscalding.
2. Oily flavour can result from overcooking.
3. Insipid cream can result from undercooking.
4. Very pale cream (it should be straw coloured) can result if too acid, or over-ripened milk is used, i.e. over 0.21 acidity.

5. Gritty textured cream results from overscalded cream.
6. Insufficiently granular cream, i.e. too smooth and bland, results from underscalding.

CREAM RECIPES

Quite often cream need only be whipped and eaten or served with a dish to add a little luxury to a meal. Whipping cream properly is quite an art (see p 49) and it is worth remembering that pasteurized cream will not go sour, merely putrid, so if you want the special taste of slightly fermented cream which is so characteristic of many French dishes you must use fresh cream.

Crème Fraîche

This is a French term for a double cream which has undergone a slight fermentation and acquired a special taste. If you get to like this taste you will never want sweet cream with e.g. raspberries or strawberries again. I have never found it marketed in England but have often created a substitute by using one part soured cream to two parts double cream. I have heard that one part of cultured buttermilk (see p 76) can be used with two parts double cream just as effectively but have never tried it.

Fontainbleau

If you like the slightly fermented taste of crème fraîche you will love Fontainbleau. It is very popular in France where it is classed as a cheese. It is, however, very much on the borderline between cream and cream cheese and is such a natural progression from crème fraîche that I include it here.

$\frac{1}{2}$ pint (275ml) double cream (unpasteurized, you are relying on natural fermentation)
2 oz. (50g) very fresh milk
1 dessertspoonful of castor or vanilla sugar

Put the cream in a bowl and leave for 2-3 days. You want the natural fermentation to take place but to stop short of the cream's 'going off'. Common sense will tell you when. You can alternatively keep the cream in the fridge and just bring it out to ripen at the end. If in doubt, keep tasting it. When you want to serve it, sprinkle the sugar over the cream and start to whip, adding the fresh milk little by little. Whip until it piles up nicely but do not overwhip or it will be buttery. It is indescribably delicious eaten with fresh fruit.

Crémets d'Angers
Once again these overlap with the cheese section. They are small heart-shaped creams, so lovely that they can make a pudding course alone, or are suitable as an extra special accompaniment for fruit.

They are very simple to make. Whip ½ pint (275ml) of cream and then, separately, whip 2 egg whites as for soufflés and fold them into the cream. Have a sterile muslin cloth to line each little heart-shaped mould. (Heart-shaped moulds fitted with drainage holes, can be obtained in some shops in England but a good alternative are small wicker baskets – after all the word 'fromage' derives from the Greek *formos* meaning 'rush basket'. This is interesting as it shows a continuing use of such baskets in Mediterranean cheese-making. Our word 'cheese' incidentally derives from the Latin *caseus* as do the words for cheese in German, Dutch, Irish, Welsh and even Spanish.) Coming back to the crémets, stand them on something to drain and leave in a cool place until the next day. Do not refrigerate as this spoils the essential flavour, serve covered with whipped cream.

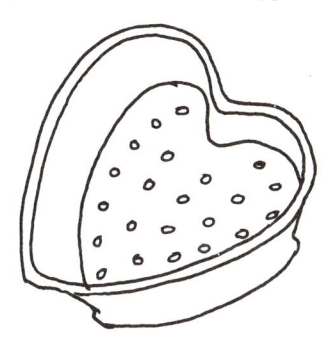

Figure 7. Mould for Coeur à la Crème or Crémets d'Angers

These are very similar to coeur à la crème, but as this does use curd, I have included it in the cheese section (see p 111).

Crème Chantilly
This is just cream whipped up with icing sugar – not too much or it will make the cream watery. It should be whipped into a huge pile and

served with fruit. Whipping cream is the best consistency. If it is necessary to keep the cream long I believe gum arabic can be incorporated into it, but I have never done this.

Whisky Cream Crowdie
The term crowdie is a Scots one and usually involves oatmeal. To make this cream you need:
1 pint (550ml) stiffly whipped cream
2 tablespoonsful of honey
4 tablespoonsful of oatmeal
1 measure of whisky

Stir all the ingredients carefully into the whipped cream, adding the whisky last. It can also be frozen and makes ice-cream crowdie.

Brown Bread Cream
1 pint (550ml) double cream
3 oz. (75g) brown breadcrumbs dried in the oven
1 teaspoonful of vanilla essence
1 measure brandy
1 pint (550ml) strawberries or stoned cherries in liqueur.

Whip the cream, fold in the breadcrumbs and then lightly stir in first the vanilla then the brandy. Spoon into dishes and arrange the fruit around the outside.

Mont Blanc
1 lb (450g) chestnuts
$\frac{1}{2}$ lb (225g) castor sugar
$\frac{1}{2}$ pint (275ml) double cream.

Shell the chestnuts and boil in a mixture of water and milk until soft. Drain and sieve them with most of the sugar, letting them fall very lightly through the sieve into the dish in which they will be served. Whip the cream with the rest of the sugar until it thickens and then pile it over the top of the chestnuts so that it looks like a snowy mountain peak. Tinned chestnut *purée* can be used, if well whipped, but does not have the light and fluffy texture of the real thing.

Syllabub

This eighteenth century dish has become quite fashionable again (although one does come across some awful concoctions served in its name in some restaurants!).

1 pint (550ml) thick cream
½ pint (275ml) sherry
2 oz. (50g) castor sugar
Juice and grated rind of a lemon

Chill a large bowl and put all the ingredients into it. Have ready chilled individual glasses. Whip all the ingredients lightly and consistently and keep skimming the foam off and filling the individual glasses with it. This makes for a delightfully light and frothy syllabub. For a more solid version whip the cream first and fold the other ingredients into it.

Mon Ami

This is an old recipe for a pudding which is part syllabub and part custard.

> 'To make mon amy, take and boile cow's creme and when it is boiled set it aside and let it cool and then take cow's crude and press out the whey then bray them together in a mortair and cast them into pots to the creme and boil together.
>
> Put thereto sugar honey and colour all with saffron and in the setting down put in yolks of egg well beet and do away the srayninge and let the potage be standing and put in dishes and plant there flowers of violetts and serve it.'
>
> Andrew Borde 1542

1 pint (550ml) thick cream
4 oz. (100g) cottage cheese
2 oz. (50g) castor sugar
4 teaspoonsful honey
10 oz. (275g) softened butter
4 egg yolks
Pinch saffron
Rose petals, crystallized violets etc.

Boil the cream and set aside, beat up the cottage cheese and mix with the sugar, honey, saffron and cream. Blend well, beat in softened butter (in small pieces) and egg yolks, place in a saucepan and heat gently stirring until thickened. *Do not boil.* Put into decorative individual glasses and decorate tops of each with crystallized violets, rose petals or something similar.

Custards
Baked custards made with cream are extremely delicious. They are made as milk custards (see p 35) but require even slower and more careful cooking. Use a bain-marie, or double saucepan. Flavour very delicately with flower waters or almonds.

Crème Brûlée
This is one of the most delicious puddings that exists. It is really only a baked custard with a caramelized sugar topping and is easy to make but has a very professional finish to it. The contrast between the crisp toffee crust and the creamy interior appeals to almost everyone.

1 pint (550ml) cream
5 egg yolks
2 oz. (50g) castor sugar (or vanilla sugar)
Vanilla pod
6 oz. (175g) demerara sugar for the topping

Scald the cream and vanilla pod in a bain-marie. Remove the pod and allow to cool. Beat yolks and castor sugar together, stir in the cream little by little and return the mixture to the bain-marie. Cook slowly stirring all the time, do not allow to boil. When the mixture can coat the back of a spoon it is the right consistency and can be poured into a dish or individual pots. Stand these in a baking dish of water and bake at about 350°F (177°C, gas mark 4) until cooked (for about 30 minutes).

Keep the pots covered with tinfoil while baking. It does not matter too much if the custard is a bit runny – it is better this way than over-set. Allow them to cool and then sprinkle the tops so that all the custard is well covered with demerara sugar. Place them in a grill tray of water and put under a pre-heated grill or salamander until the sugar begins to bubble and turn dark brown. (If you are an Aga user and have no grill as such, a blow-torch comes in handy. We keep a butane gas blow-torch specially for finishing a lot of dishes which need a brown top, it makes visitors to our kitchen laugh but does the job quite adequately.)

Chill and serve. If you freeze the toffee it tends to lose its crisp bite.

The custard can be made the day before and the toffee put on the day of serving but allow enough time to cool well.

Almond Creams
This is very similar to crème brulée but has a nut topping rather than a toffee one.
1 pint (550ml) cream
5 egg yolks
2 oz. (50g) castor sugar
4 oz. (100g) ground almonds
Blanched, or roasted blanched almonds to finish.

Scald the cream in a bain-marie. Mix the eggs, sugar and ground almonds together. Add the cooked cream to this mixture and return to saucepan to cook (without boiling of course) until thickened. Stir all the time and when it reaches the consistency at which it will coat a spoon, pour into the pots. Stand in baking dish of water and cook until set (about 30 minutes at 350°F, 177°C, gas mark 4). Chill and decorate with the whole almonds.

Real Ice-Cream
Real ice-cream, made from your own cream, is far superior to the shop bought stuff which (as the EEC commissioners, rightly for once, pointed out) does not contain cream at all. It is worth keeping a dairy animal for this alone.

If you become an ice-cream addict (and it is very easy to do so as the variety is almost limitless and the procedure not difficult) it is well worth buying an electric ice-cream maker. These machines plug into an electric socket and stand inside the freezing compartment of the fridge; the flex shuts in the door quite easily and the power works a paddle which keeps the ice cream at just the right consistency. There are several makes available and the prices are very reasonable if you plan to take up ice-cream making seriously. Made thus the ice-cream will be ready in a couple of hours. Some models have paddles which lift after the mixture has reached the right consistency, making it easier to unmould the finished ice-cream when it has hardened.

If you do not have an ice-cream maker, you can still make your own ice-cream but the process will take longer and be more laborious because in order to prevent ice-granules forming and spoiling the texture of the ice-cream, you must remove it from the freezer compartment or freezer at least once during the freezing process and whip thoroughly. The results will not, even so, be as smooth as the gentle blending that the machine achieves. Another way is to take the mixture out fairly frequently and stir it well as it freezes, which does prolong the process but gives a fairly smooth end result.

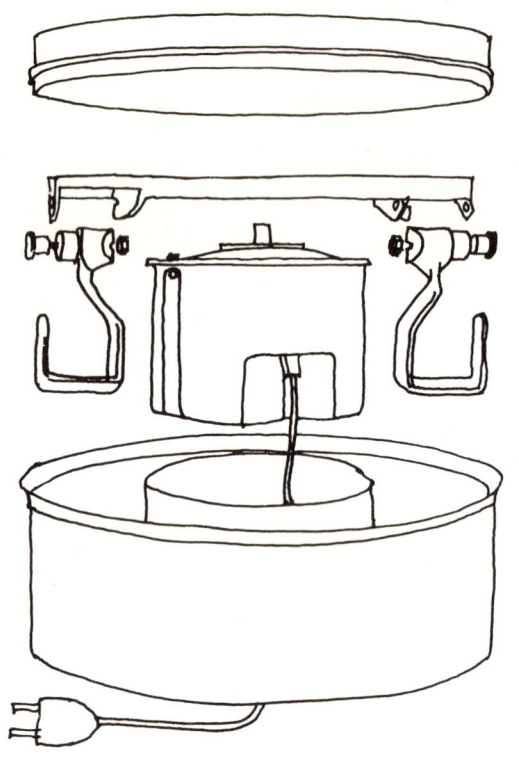

Figure 8. Ice-cream maker

Real ice-cream is not just a mixture of frozen cream and flavouring, it is or should be frozen custard, preferably a rich custard made with cream, flavouring and egg yolks. The flavouring can be almost anything and needs to be fairly strong as anything tastes less potent when frozen. Similarly it should be well sweetened.

Vanilla Dairy Ice-cream
This is the basic custard. For alternatives instead of vanilla use flavourings suggested below.
1 cupful of milk
6 oz. (175g) castor sugar
8 egg yolks beaten
Vanilla pod
1 pint (550ml) cream (double)

Heat milk, vanilla pod, sugar and pour onto the egg yolks stirring all the time. Return the mixture to the pan and cook gently in bain-marie or double saucepan, until custard thickens. Allow to cool, take out vanilla pod and then fold in the cream. Freeze, either in freezer compartment of fridge or in a deep freeze. As mentioned above, in order to achieve a creamy texture the mixture must either be stirred as it freezes to prevent ice-crystals forming or, half way through the process, it must be thoroughly whipped.

Fruit Ice-cream
Add any of the following to your basic recipe just before the freezing stage.
Strawberries. Wild strawberry is probably the most delicious, although any fresh berry fruit is very tasty. Liquidize the fruit or make a *purée* of it. It is necessary to sweeten it with very tart fruit as freezing tends to make things taste less sweet. Fold in cream and freeze.
Peaches or any Firm Fruit. Remove skin, core or stone and cut in pieces and simmer with sugar to soften. Then *purée* or liquidize and add to basic custard as before. Fold in cream and freeze.
Citrus Fruit. Although these are better known as sorbets or water ices, they can be used to make cream ices too. Add the juice and the finely grated skin of oranges, lemons or grapefruit (avoiding pips or pith) and add extra sugar to the custard mixture, then fold in cream and freeze.
Mango, Melon, Pineapple. These can be *puréed* or liquidized as with soft berry fruit. *Banana* can be mashed or *puréed*.
Very Lazy Ice-cream. This is really a disgrace, but useful for those days when time runs out! 1 pint (550ml) packet custard, made up, (or even worse, a can of it) combined with 1 pint (550ml) double cream softly whipped. Fold together and freeze.

Moka
This is rather a superior coffee ice-cream. Bruise ¾ lb (350g) roasted coffee beans in a mortar. Put these in a saucepan with 1 pint (550ml) single cream, yolks of 3 eggs, 3 oz (75g) of soft brown sugar and a piece of lemon peel. Cook this custard until it thickens and then strain out the coffee beans through a sieve. When the custard is cold, fold in ¼ pint (150ml) double cream and freeze in the usual way.

Chocolate Ice-cream
Blend melted (but cooled) chocolate into the custard. Fold a little *grated* chocolate in with the cream for texture. Any sort of chocolate can be used, bitter, cooking, swiss, milk or plain. Alternatively mix some chocolate powder with a little hot milk, cool and add to the custard.

Nut Ices
Any sort of nut can be added either on its own or as a texture for other flavours. If you have a liquidizer you can vary the texture and add some very finely ground nuts for flavour and some more coarsely ground nuts for texture. Hazelnut is delicious, especially with caramel (see below).

Some More Suggestions
Jams, honey, fruit syrup and *marmalade* can all be used to flavour ices and to make a 'ripple'.
Caramel can be simply made by dissolving 4 oz. (100g) sugar in a little water until it bubbles and turns brown. Add this at the hot custard stage.
Maple syrup can be used similarly and makes another very good ice.
Flower water, rose or orange blossom (which is available from Middle Eastern grocers) make subtly flavoured ice-cream. Especially good is rose water together with some crystallized rose petals.
Mint ice is very cooling. Add 2 tablespoonsful of crème de menthe and the equivalent of a small bunch of liquified or finely chopped fresh mint. This may benefit from the addition of a few drops of food colouring.
Blue Ice-cream can be made from the basic recipe with the addition of 2 tablespoonsful of blue curaço and some blue colouring.
If you like alcoholic ices, brandy, whisky, rum, vermouth or sherry can be added but it is more fun to use liqueurs (and they can be

bought by the miniature). A combination of marmalade and grand marnier for example is absolutely delicious. Really with ice cream your experiments can be great fun and you can make use of anything in your cupboard from glacé cherries to digestive biscuits.

Before leaving the subject of puddings, I should like to include one more recipe using cream.

Clafoutis
2 eggs
3 oz. (75g) sugar
1½ oz. (40g) flour
¼ pint (150ml) double cream
1 lb (450g) stoned cherries
1 tot of kirsch

Cream the eggs and the sugar in a basin with an electric whisk (otherwise beat hard). Add the flour and the kirsch and beat thoroughly. Fold in the cream. Put the cherries in an earthen ware shallow oven dish and pour the rich batter over. Cook in a preheated oven at 350°F (177°C gas mark 4) for about 35 minutes. The top should be golden brown but the inside should be custardy. Can be eaten hot or cold with plenty of cream, preferably a large dish of crème chantilly.

Cream in Sauces
Cream enriches sauces making a meal much more luxurious and can be added to a basic béchamel.
Sauce Mousseline. This is simply Hollondaise Sauce with the addition of thick whipped cream.
Sauce Messine. This is delicious with poached fish or hard boiled eggs.
1 pint (550ml) fresh cream (single)
2 oz. (50g) unsalted butter
1 teaspoonful of flour
2 egg yolks
2-3 shallots
A lemon, chervil, parsley and tarragon and some french mustard.

Chop the herbs and shallots together with a little lemon peel. Work the butter and the flour together and add the mustard, the beaten egg yolks and cream. Blend with the herb and shallot mixture and put into a double saucepan. Stir gently until the sauce thickens. Do not let it boil. Add the lemon juice just before serving.

Stroganoff Sauce
This is a sour cream sauce. For one pint (550ml) of sour cream soften 2 oz. (50g) of sliced button mushrooms and 1 small onion in butter. Add $\frac{1}{2}$ teaspoonful of tomato *purée*, stir in the sour cream, heat and serve.

Sour cream can be blended with french mustard and a little vinegar, salt and pepper for use with mackerel or cold salt beef. It can also be blended with tomato *purée* (or ketchup) and a dash of worcestershire sauce for use with shellfish.

Cream improves any *purée* type soup. As with butter, add the cream at the last moment just as the soup is to be served. Stir the soup in the tureen or plate and then add the cream so that it makes a whirl.

5
BUTTER

Constituents

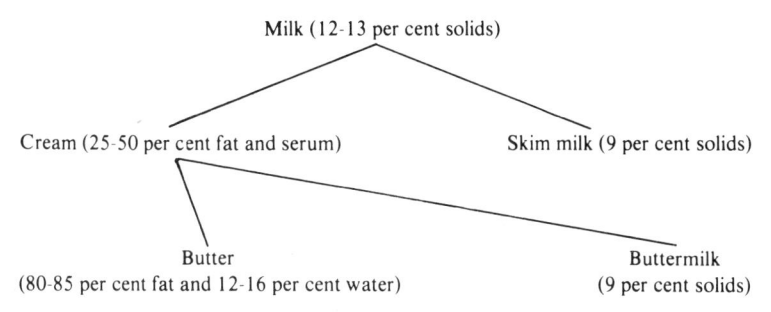

```
                    Milk (12-13 per cent solids)
                   /                            \
Cream (25-50 per cent fat and serum)      Skim milk (9 per cent solids)
        \
         \
          \
       Butter                              Buttermilk
(80-85 per cent fat and 12-16 per cent water)    (9 per cent solids)
```

Figure 9. Division of milk constituents into butter

Although the percentages above are not exact, they serve to show the approximate proportions of the constituents of milk when separated into cream and skim. The cream is further processed to make butter in which the oil in water emulsion of milk changes into the water in oil emulsion of butter.

Butter can be made from the whole milk but is more usually made from cream. The best butter is made from cream of around 30 per cent butterfat. If heavier it tends to coat the inside of the churn with a fatty layer which cushions the impact on the fat globules. For it is a characteristic of cream that when shaken or agitated the fat globules coalesce into larger and larger lumps. If the cream is too light the excess water acts as a barrier to the formation of the butter.

For separation see p 47. If you are using goat's milk, you will need a separator.

Equipment
Anything in which the cream can be placed and agitated violently can serve as a churn.

64 MAKING CHEESES, BUTTERS, CREAM AND YOGURT

Electric butter churns are very efficient but expensive. If you are dealing with large amounts of cream and can afford it, this is the quickest method.

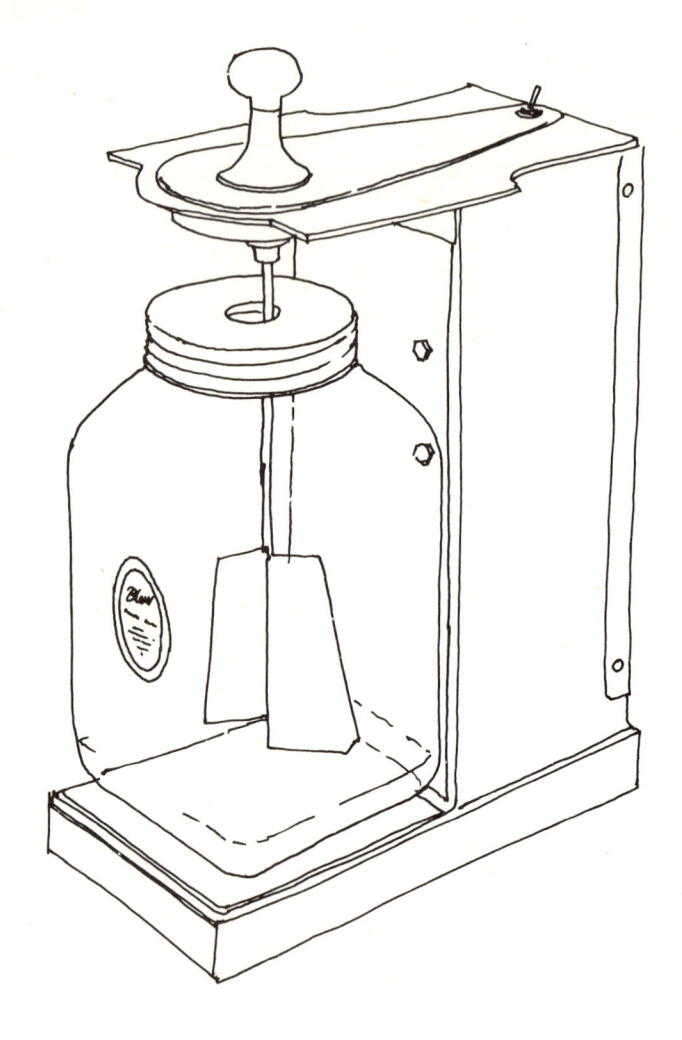

Figure 10. Electric butter churn

Hand churns. The Blow glass jar type churn is extremely good value. The churns are listed by capacity of cream and spare jars are available. This is the most universally used churn if you are preparing a domestic butter supply of not too large an amount.

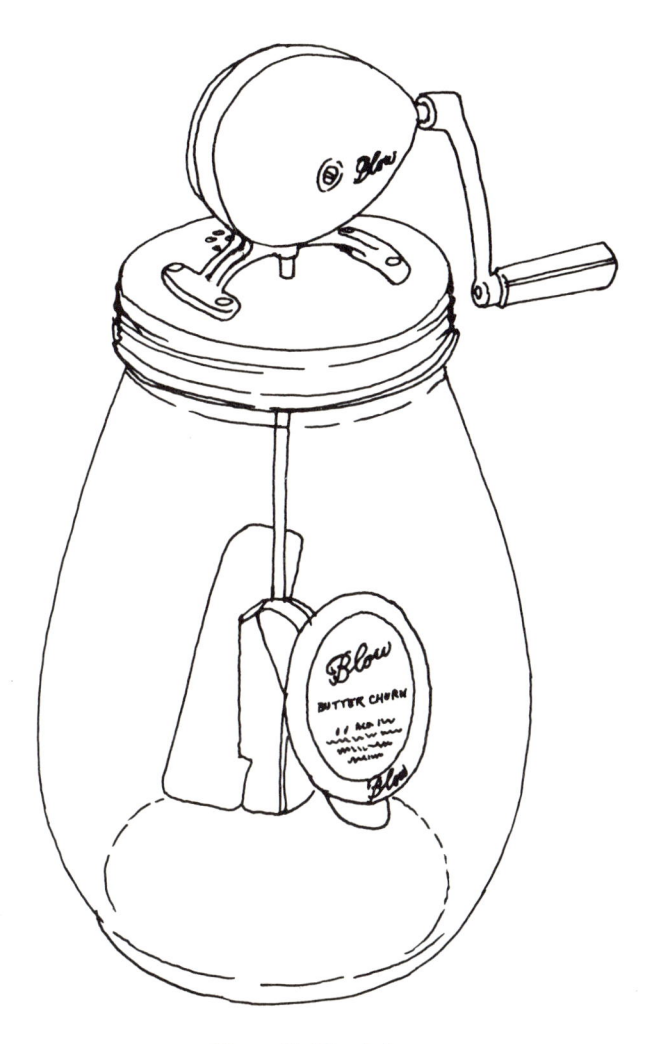

Figure 11. Hand churn

Up-and-over churns. I have one of these traditional churns and I find it most satisfying to use. They are not manufactured any more as far as I know but with the increased interest in self-sufficiency perhaps someone will start making them again.

Electric mixer. It is quite possible to churn in an ordinary electric mixer. The secret is to fill the mixer less than half full and to begin fairly fast and then to slow down (unles you want the butter to splatter all over you and the kitchen) as you progress. As soon as the butter begins to break, turn off and work the butter.

A large glass jar which you can shake about will do, but you will find it rather a lengthy process.

A bowl and spoon can be used, the spoon simply bashing the cream about until it coalesces. This is also long and tiring.

Butter worker. This is a tray type device equipped with a draining hole and is used in conjunction with a corrugated rolling pin. It is not essential for butter making but does make the job of expelling the surplus water easier. As an alternative

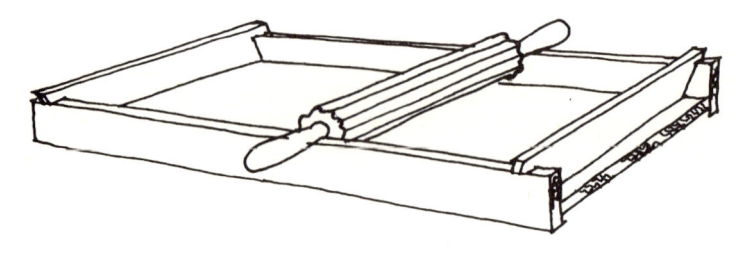

Figure 12. Butter worker

A wooden board and a pair of *scotch hands* may be used to work the butter. The scotch hands are very important and a good heavy pair is an investment.

Moulds. Attractive moulds in which the butter can be shaped and which impress a design on the butter make for a good 'finish'.

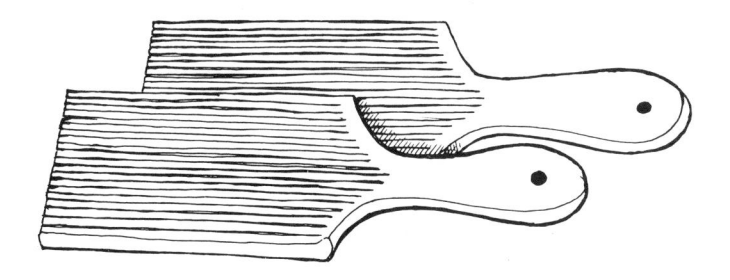

Figure 13. Scotch hands

Butter-making

If you only have the milk from one cow or goat, you will want to save up the cream until you have enough to make the butter-making operation worthwhile.

Place the cream from each meal into a large receptacle which you will fill bit by bit. Each time you put some more in, stir thoroughly. A gallon of cream yields about 4 lb (about 2kg) of butter. If you have a fridge you need only make butter once a week. In summer you will probably need to make it twice a week – traditionally butter-making took place twice a week and never on a Sunday.

When you have added the last batch of cream remove the receptacle from the fridge. The cream can either be churned 'sweet' or ripened. Cream will not ripen below 50°F (10°C) and fermentations other than the required lactic acid can cause off flavours. The cream must then be left for 12 hours to ripen. Ripened cream is that which is slightly soured and this makes for butter of a better flavour, as exposure to the air for some time causes oxygen to unite with some of the fatty acids and produce lactic acid. *Sweet Cream* butter, although rather more insipid, has always had its adherents. Stevens in his famous *Book of the Farm* in 1870 said,

> 'For my own I would never desire better all the year round than that churned new every morning from sweet cream. Such a butter accompanied by a cup of strong coffee modified by crystallized sugar and fresh cream, is a breakfast worth partaking of.'

In fact most of the butter produced commercially is sweet cream butter which has been pasteurized and artificially aged under refrigeration before being put in the churn or 'continuous butter-maker' as it is known in commercial terms.

Lactic Butter or Ripened Cream Butter

You can, if you wish pasteurize the cream and add a starter as is done commercially but for the small-holder it is quite adequate to remove the container from the fridge some 12 hours before churning is to begin. This is usually enough for 'natural ripening' to take place i.e. for the lactic acid to get to work. The ideal acidity is 0.5-0.6 which you can check if you have an acidimeter. If you wish to ripen the cream artificially bring the temperature to 60-64°F (15-17°C) and add some sour milk, sour cream or buttermilk.

Temperature

Temperature is critical in butter-making and a dairy thermometer is really a very good investment. The correct starting temperature depends a lot on the season, the ripeness of the cream and the ambient temperature.

It can be altered by standing the vessel on the edge of the stove and stirring. If you are dealing with large amounts you can immerse a temperature can i.e. a can full of boiling water, in the cream, and raise the temperature that way.

Room Temp.	Churning Temp.
18°C (66°F)	11°C (52°F)
14°C (57°F)	13°C (56°F)
10°C (50°F)	15°C (59°F)

Figure 14. Suggested churning temperatures depending on room temperature

Never bring the temperature of cream above 80°F (27°C). Test the cream at least 3 hours before churning so that any adjustments can be made gradually. At the same time check that all the utensils are scrupulously clean. (Do it in advance so that they have cooled down properly.) Rinse with cold water, scald to sterilize, stand upside down to air. If you are using a butter worker, wrap the roller in sterilized damp muslin.

BUTTER

Colouring

If you wish to colour your butter you can add some 12 drops of annatto per gallon. Annatto is a dye derived from the seed of the *Bixa orellana* from the West Indies. It is dissolved in refined vegetable oil and so colours butter (and cheese) but not the buttermilk. Add the annatto as you pour the cream into the churn. Perfectionists strain the cream through muslin to ensure even consistency. Do not fill the churn more than half full. Begin to churn slowly and increase speed. If the churn is fitted with a valve, depress it from time to time to release gases. The butter will take anything from 1-5 minutes if electrically churned or 20-30 minutes if hand churned to 'break' or 'come'. When it does the cream separates irreversibly into buttermilk and little yellow pellets of butter.

Some firms market butter colourer under the name of 'Oleo' to distinguish it from the annatto used for cheese colouring.

Problems

If after 40 minutes there is still just white cream in the churn:
1. The cream may be too cold. Try opening the churn and throwing in a cupful (less if churn is small) of hot water.
2. The surrounding atmosphere may be too warm and the cream 'sleepy' i.e. sticking to the sides of the churn. Try adding some icy cold water. See that there is good ventilation and churn slowly.
3. Frothiness in the churn may be due to the cream's being too thin or improperly ripened.

If all else fails, open the churn, take out the cream, scald it and begin all over again!

Washing

As soon as the butter breaks, drain off the buttermilk and put it to one side. If the diary animal is from an interesting pasture it can make a lovely drink. It is also useful for cooking and can be made into cheese (see p 76).

Add plenty of cold water (technically it should be 2°F colder than the temperature in the churn) to the butter in the churn in order to wash it. The quantity is about a quart (about 1 litre) to each original gallon ($4\frac{1}{2}$ litres). Churn slowly and drain. Repeat this procedure until the water is clear. The object is to remove all the buttermilk because this is, and should be, sour, whereas the butter must not contain a hint of it or it will go rancid. Overwashing does tend to remove the flavour and the secret is to know when the right amount of buttermilk has been washed out. At first it is advisable to err a little on the side of overwashing rather than the other way round.

Salting
It is possible to salt butter in the churn, or even by giving the butter a last wash in brine but it is more usual to incorporate the salting into the next procedure below.

Working
Remove the butter from the churn and place it on the butter worker or on a *clean* wooden board (not one you have just chopped onions on!). Leave it to drain (if using board tip it up) for 15 minutes. Then work the whole mass together with the roller or scotch hands. Then weigh it for salting. Salting is a very personal thing, I prefer the merest hint of salt in butter while others like it really salt. Try about $\frac{1}{4}$-$\frac{1}{2}$ oz. (6-12g) salt per 1 lb (450g). Sprinkle the salt on and leave for another 15 minutes to dissolve, so that the butter will not end up too streaky. Then roll out thinly removing the water with the sterile muslin, and fold into a sausage or swiss roll shape. Keep doing this until all the water has been removed. The legal limit is 16 per cent water and the more you can remove the less chance there is of rancidity developing. When you have worked the butter leave it for a while to harden up before the final stage.

Making Up
The butter can be worked into blocks, rounds, squares or rolls with the scotch hands. If you find a decorative mould, this adds a finish to the butter. Wrap the butter very carefully as light and air oxydize the unsaturated fatty acids and cause rancidity. Butter keeps in a freezer for months.

Possible Faults
Sourness. This is due to overripe (i.e. sour) cream or insufficient buttermilk being removed.
Leaky butter. This is due to too much salt being added.
Streaky butter. This is caused by overchurning, insufficient washing or badly mixed salt.

Mottled butter. If butter has an oily mottled appearance it may be because the cream was overripe.

Tainted tasting butter. If butter is tainted because of something the cow has eaten (p 18) try sweetening it as for rancid butter but if the cow is still on the offending pasture, scald the cream next time before you begin. Stand the pan in boiling water and when a wrinkle appears on the cream remove to a temperature of 50°F (10°C).

If the butter is tainted from an external source make sure that the board you used for working the butter was absolutely clean and sweet smelling. Often these taints can be traced to last night's garlic! There is a small dairy mould called *odium lactic* which invades the wood of old dairies and can give the produce a strange fishy taste. It is rare and only found in old dairies. Remember that poorly cleaned utensils spoil more dairy products than anything else.

To Sweeten Rancid Butter

1. Wash and mash in new milk, rinse and rinse again.
2. Beat in lime water (I have never tried this) and rinse.
3. Place in a pan with a little water, bring to the boil and skim. A few pieces of toasted bread dropped in are said to absorb the taste and odour. Cool, drain and set. Or, similarly pour on boiling water, melt all together in a pan and leave to cool, drain off water and set. If you heat butter, you drive off the volatile fats which may be causing the rancidity but you are not left with real butter any more. What you have is a sort of ghee, very much used in Indian cooking and in no way to be despised. Certainly useful in cooking once you have got rid of the off-odours.

To make ghee simmer butter in a pan for an hour, skim off any scum and keep in an airtight container.

Other Methods of Preserving Butter

Well washed butter will keep for a month in the fridge and will keep for months in a freezer. If you have no fridge tiny quantities can be kept fresh by placing on an earthenware dish in a cool place and covering with a strip of muslin, the ends of which dip into containers of cold water.

Larger quantities can be preserved in a crock or 'potted' with a fairly high proportion of salt. Salt at the rate of about $2\frac{1}{2}$ per cent its weight. Scald a crock, tub or barrel and air dry. Throw the butter hard into the vessel to exclude air, then add a handful of salt. Continue until the crock is full to the top. Cover well and keep away from strong odours which could taint the butter. When you come to use this butter you may have to wash some of the salt out of it.

Pickled butter is another effective means of preserving butter. Make a pickle from 1 quart (about 1 litre) boiling water, 2 lbs (about 1kg) salt and 3 oz. (75g) loaf sugar and 1 oz. (25g) saltpetre. Let it stand until cold and put into a large jar. Place the butter in the pickle. It is said to keep butter sweet through the hottest summer months, but I have never tried it.

USING BUTTER

French Butters
There are many classic butters in the French cuisine.

Montpellier Butter
This is served with salmon. Plunge a few tarragon, chive, chervil and spinach leaves into boiling water for 1 minute. Drain and dry in a cloth. Chop up finely and add 2 tablespoonsful of chopped capers, 6 anchovy fillets (if not packed in oil, wash to remove excess salt) a clove of garlic, 6 hard boiled egg yolks, 8 oz. (225g) butter and 2 tablespoonsful of wine vinegar. Add these chopped ingredients little by little and blend very thoroughly.

Beurre Blanc
This is served in France with pike or shad. Simmer 2 very finely chopped shallots with $\frac{1}{2}$ glassful of wine vinegar. Reduce this to about 1 tablespoonful of liquid, cool, and whisk in 2-3 oz. (50-75g) butter little by little. The butter must not melt but must have a creamy consistency. This should be made from slightly salted butter, not overchurned, and wine vinegar from muscadet wine! It is heresy to add cream to the finished product and apparently took one of the great chefs 15 tries before he got it right.

Beurre Marchand de Vin
This is similar to the butter above but wine is used instead of vinegar. Reduce a tablespoonful of chopped shallots in $\frac{1}{4}$ pint (150ml) of red

wine until about 1 tablespoonful of liquid is left. Cool and beat in 2-3 oz. (50-75g) of butter as above. A little meat glaze can be added too.

Beurre Bercy
This is the same as Marchand de Vin but uses white wine.

Beurre Maître d'Hôtel
One to use with steaks, fish etc. Take a heaped tablespoonful of chopped parsley and beat it into 3 oz. (75g) unsalted butter, season lightly with salt and freshly ground pepper and add the juice of $\frac{1}{2}$ a lemon. Mix all together very thoroughly. Do not heat or melt this butter but place portions of it on hot plates and serve the steak, fish etc. on top of it.

Beurre Colbert
This is maître d'hôtel with the addition of chopped tarragon, and a dash of meat glaze. (If you grow your own herbs you will know that you have to be careful to use the French tarragon as the other types grow huge but have no taste.)

Herb Butters

If you do grow herbs an alternative short-term method of preserving them, other than drying them, is to make some little pots of herb butters which will last quite well in the fridge. These can be brought out for use as garnishes for fish and steak dishes, flavourings for omelettes and for use in sandwiches. Sandwiches seem to conjure a rather tired and banal image but by using savoury or herb butters quite a new dimension can be added. The butter acts not only as a damp proofer but can be selected to complement the filling. A knob of tarragon butter with steak or chicken is delicious as is a pat of fennel butter with fish or swirled into potato or carrot soup. Almost any herb can be used.

Green Butter
Scald one or two green chives, a few spinach leaves, some parsley, tarragon or chervil (i.e. some or all of these). Drain well and pound. Work in 2 oz. (50g) butter and season. A little green colouring can be added if desired.

Caper Butter
Blend 2 tablespoonsful of chopped capers with 1 oz. (25g) butter. Can be spread in a layer and fish served on top or can be made up into pats and used on fish.

Tomato Butter
Use the pulp of fresh tomatoes or a little tomato *purée*, blend with butter and add a pinch of paprika.

Mustard Butter
Excellent with ham, pork or sausages. Blend mustard (French, English or German) with butter at the rate of about $1\frac{1}{2}$ oz. (40g) of butter to a teaspoonful of mustard. Once again your taste will dictate how hot you make it.

Garlic Butter
Pound garlic and mix with butter. Spread thickly over french bread and heat for a few minutes in the oven.

Worcester Butter
Grate a little cheese very finely and add a few drops of worcestershire sauce. Blend with the butter adding maybe a hint of grated onions.

Anchovy Butter
Wash a couple of anchovies well and remove any bones, pound with fresh butter and a squeeze of lemon juice. Slip into the body of a grilled fish.

Lobster Butter
Sprinkle the spawn and coral of lobster with cayenne pepper (not too much) add double the amount of butter and blend well.

Butter in Cooking
As butter is heated the water content is driven off and the butter foams after which it turns light brown, dark brown and finally burns. Each of the stages up to burning are made use of in cooking.

Beurre Noisette
This is butter at the golden stage, with a dash of lemon juice added. It is poured over sizzling fish and is very good.

BUTTER

Black Butter
This is a deep mahogany coloured butter. Fry a tablespoonful of parsley finely chopped or minced, in 2 oz. (50g) butter until it reaches the right colour. Stir in 1 tablespoonful of vinegar and pour over skate or other fish.

Clarified Butter
Both the above sorts of butter can be made with clarified butter and many recipes call for it. Butter is heated until frothy, the froth is then skimmed off and the resulting clear yellow liquid is strained through a muslin and put in a jar. There will be a milky deposit in the bottom of the pan. In clarifying butter the salt, casein and lactose are removed and the resulting butter will not burn easily. It also has good keeping qualities but loses a lot of volume.

Beurre Manié
Mash together an equal quantity of butter and flour, squeeze in palm of hand to combine. It can be used to thicken soups and stews but must not boil fast.

Sweet Butters
Just as in savoury or herb butters, honey, nuts or fruit can be blended with butter for sandwiches etc. The best known sweet butter is probably brandy butter.

Brandy Butter
The usual accompaniment to Christmas Pudding in Great Britain. Beat 3 oz. (75g) butter to a cream and add 2 tablespoonsful of icing sugar and a few drops of vanilla essence. Then add brandy until the mixture will absorb no more while remaining stiff.

Cumberland Rum Butter
This is an alternative for Christmas time and is simply made by working together 4 oz. (100g) sweet butter, 4 oz. (100g) castor sugar (or vanilla sugar) $\frac{1}{4}$ tablespoonful of grated lemon peel, $\frac{1}{4}$ teaspoonful of cinnamon and as much rum as the mixture will hold (about 4 tablespoonsful).

Butter Creams
There are several ways of making butter cream for icing and filling cakes. They can be given various flavourings, for example strong

coffee or orange juice. (see section on ice-cream).

This is one to make in an electric mixer if you have one. If not it is hard work. Run the mixer bowl under hot water and dry it then beat together 2 egg yolks, 2 oz. (50g) of icing sugar and 6 oz. (175g) of unsalted butter. Add any flavouring and blend for about 5 minutes or until really smooth.

Butter can be added to a cooked, cooled custard base, or into a meringue type base made with whipped egg whites to give a different texture.

BUTTERMILK

Buttermilk is a by-product from butter-making but has a lot of character itself and can provide a good deal of extra nourishment for you. It can of course be fed to stock who benefit from its protein but here are a few suggestions for the family.

As a Drink

The flavour depends entirely on the flavour of the butter which in turn depends on the ripeness of the cream, the pasture of the cows and the stage in the lactation. At one time it was chilled and served as a drink and was highly thought of. Now we tend to prefer 'cultured' buttermilk which is milder in flavour and creamier in consistency.

Straight buttermilk can be used in mashed potatoes or baking.

To Culture Your own Buttermilk

Warm 2 pints (about 1 litre) of milk to 90°F (32°C), add 1 cupful of buttermilk and incubate at a temperature of 70°F (21°C) until thickened. Then chill.

Crempog – Welsh Pancakes

Sieve 6 oz. (175g) of plain flour into a bowl and rub in 1 oz (25g) of butter. Mix sufficient buttermilk to make a smooth batter. Beat up an egg and stir in. Leave covered for 3 hours. Prepare a pan with hot fat and just before frying stir in a ½ teaspoonful of bicarbonate of soda. Coat the pan very thinly with the batter to make a lot of thin light pancakes.

Buttermilk Scones

Scones are much nicer if buttermilk or cultured buttermilk is used in place of fresh milk.

Curds and Whey

Scald ½ pint (275ml) of creamy milk and stir in 1 pint of buttermilk. Leave to stand until the curd has formed (if too loose, heat gently to reduce curd). Cool thoroughly. Tip into a cloth to drain and when crumbly pat into shapes. Dredge these individually with vanilla sugar and pour thick cream over them. The whey is traditionally flavoured or sweetened and served separately in a jug as a sauce.

Hatted Kit

This is a recipe from about the beginning of the eighteenth century from Dorothy Hartley's *Food in England* (see *Suggested Further Reading*). A kit is a wooden pail.

Mix 2 quarts (2.3 litres) of new milk, scalding hot, and quickly with four quarts (4.5 litres) cold fresh buttermilk. Let stand until cold and firm, skim off the 'hat' and set it to drain, then press into moulds, turn out and serve with cream and sugar.

6
CHEESE-MAKING: THE TECHNIQUE

Home cheese-making is an extremely interesting and useful activity. Once the basic principles are grasped and one gains confidence one can experiment not only by attempting to make well known cheeses but, and this seems to me of much more importance to the smallholder, by trying to discover and create your very own 'farmhouse' cheeses. At one time cheese-making was undertaken by each farmhouse to convert the summer flush of milk into something which would last into the leaner winter months. The type of cheese depended directly on the type of pasture, the time of year and the time in the lactation. The size of herd was also of importance and the number of cows to each 'meal' or milking dictated the number of milkings to a cheese and this in turn altered the acidity balance and thus the type as well as the size of cheese. So different farms produced different cheeses and the craft was essentially localized.

From Farm to Factory
With the advent of motor transport liquid milk was taken directly off the farms and there was no need for its conversion into something more lasting. As Dorothy Hartley says in *Food in England*, the dairymaid left her dairy for ever, riding down from the farm with the milk lorry to do the same work at the local creamery, in good company and for more money. It was the end of an era. The old farmhouse dairies with all their cheese moulds built up over the centuries, fell into disuse.

Nowadays cheese is factory produced all the year round. Milk is pasteurized and inoculated with the required 'starter' and the result is a uniform product of good shelf-life expectancy, certainly in no way to be despised but with little individuality.

Thus anyone with their own milk supply is in the fortunate position of being able to revive an almost lost art, to produce a cheese which is entirely his own and which reflects his taste, his pasture, the quality of his dairy animals' milk and the conditions in his own cheese room. Further, and this is worth considering if one reflects on the disasters

CHEESE-MAKING: THE TECHNIQUE

which dogged the poor dairymaid throughout history, it can be undertaken nowadays with the backing of knowledge based upon scientific principles. Until the last century the basis for cheese-making was purely empirical; if it worked you did it, even if you had no idea why.

An Ancient Art

This had more or less always been so; curds of some sort were probably used by nomadic tribesmen who found out about the characteristics of rennet by carrying milk in bags made from young animal skins. There are certainly biblical references to 'Cheese of Kine' in Samuel, and 10 slices of cheese were presented to the captain of the army against Saul in Samuel 18. So in ancient times cheese was made and enjoyed. Greece was exporting cheese in the first century A.D. and in Rome it was appreciated to such an extent that a Roman would use the word 'caseus' (cheese) to describe a lady of his choice. In fact Pliny, Virgil and Columella all wrote on dairy husbandry. Columella's grasp of the principles of renneting, draining, salting, storing and general dairy hygiene in cheese-making were so advanced that eighteen hundred years later in England his treatise could have been profitably studied.

Dairymaid's Disasters

The poor dairymaid was trying to produce curd without any knowledge about the micro-organisms in the milk, she was using rennet without any clear idea of what it did or what amount should be used or at what temperature. Not surprisingly she tended to produce 'slip-curd' a soft and slimy curd which would not contract and which was blamed for almost every other mishap in the making of the cheese. Even if she did managed to produce a curd, she then kneaded and squeezed it with all her might, loosing much of the richness of the cheese in the process. It was not until ripening stage however, that her real troubles began. Knowing nothing of the chemical changes which take place in the cheese as it is ripened by enzymic action, and having little regard to the proximity of dung-heaps, cesspits etc., she spent a large proportion of her time trying to rescue her cheeses from attack by rats, mice, flies, maggots, mites and the effects of strange fermentations.

Cheeses were known as 'hoven' or 'blowed', when they swelled up and burst. They would 'fly out' or bulge at the sides and they became 'wind-shook' or 'jointed'. The coats of cheeses were 'leaky', 'husky', 'spongey' and 'full of eyes' and if mice did not feast on them then probably the cheese fly would lay its eggs on them and the eggs would hatch into maggots which would eat the whole centre away. These maggots were known as 'jumpers' because they were very nimble but they could easily be joined in the same cheese by the maggots of blow flies, who were larger and slower. Possibly a plague of cheese mites, so small as to be invisible to the naked eye, might infest the cheese and reduce it within a short while to a pile of dust.

For those interested in reading about these perils, Thomas Tusser in 1572 in his poem 'Five hundred points of good husbandry and housewifery' introduces us to the poor dairymaid Cisley and as well as discussing the ills that cheeses were prone to, does a fair job in indicating the male chauvinist piggery of those days!

The Science of Cheese-making
Although developments were made in the cheese trade after this date it was the general agricultural reforms of such people as 'Turnip' Townsend, Young and Bakewell much later that led to further interest in the dairy business in particular. Yet it was not until some hundred years afterwards that Joseph Harding, with his wife and large family of expert cheese-makers, began to incorporate some of the new scientific developments into the art. Only then did cheese-making even begin to be based on the right principles. This came about to some extent because the industrial revolution, with its emphasis on machines, invaded the dairy. Such things as temperature were recognized as important and rennet was standardized and lost a lot of its old 'magical' image.

When this happened of course yields improved dramatically and cheese-making began to move from being a farmhouse activity to being a factory one. Agricultural colleges started dairying courses. Dr Lloyd with the great cheese-maker Miss Cannon did experiments which resulted in the invention of the acidimeter. The recognition of the importance of acidity levels together with the dramatic new science of microbiology soon resulted in the isolation of 'starter' bacteria which enabled cheeses to become standardized and gradeable.

Revival of Interest
From then onwards it was big business, not only in this country but in

America, France and Switzerland. Cheddar, Camembert and Emmental were no longer produced in quantity on the farm but were commercially produced in factories. While no one in their right mind would wish to return to the old days of sour, putrid and blown cheeses, there is nevertheless a mass reaction against the loss of standards that inevitably follow mass production. This dissatisfaction can be seen on many fronts; self-sufficiency, the crafts revival, the whole 'small is beautiful' ethic, underlines it. In England farmhouse cheese-making sunk as low as some 50 producers, it is now creeping up again. In France where the industrial revolution did not have the effect of causing a mass exodus from the villages to the town, the *fermier* cheeses were always well thought of and now command a higher price than similar mass-produced *laitier* items. As people travel they learn to appreciate the peasant cheeses and to respect the craft which has lead to their production. As a result those with their own milk supply can begin to take a pride in reviving such a worthwhile art, at the same time as producing something unique, something which they would be unable to find in any supermarket, something no amount of money would buy.

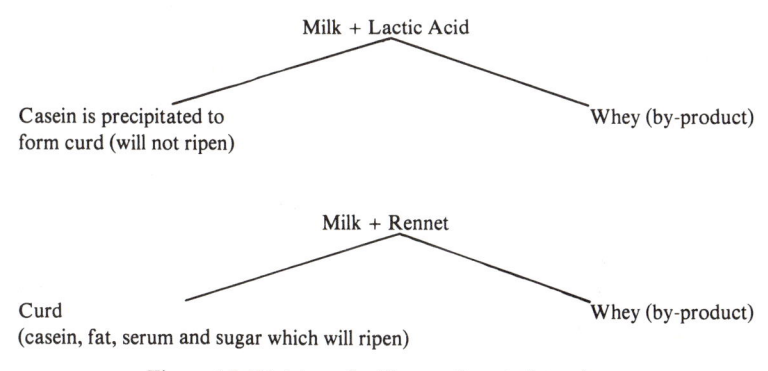

```
                    Milk + Lactic Acid
                   /                  \
Casein is precipitated to              Whey (by-product)
form curd (will not ripen)

                    Milk + Rennet
                   /              \
Curd                               Whey (by-product)
(casein, fat, serum and sugar which will ripen)
```

Figure 15. Division of milk constituents into cheese

Fermentation

An understanding of the basic principles behind the fermentation of sugars and fats is essential to successful cheese-making. There are many different micro-organisms in complex chemical changes with varying end results. However lactic fermentation, the conversion of lactose to lactic acid, is the normal process of fermentation in milk as it ages. The lactic acid causes clotting owing to the precipitation of casein when the acidity has risen to about 0.45 per cent in normal temperatures. After this the acidity will increase to 1.45 per cent when it is subsequently lost by the action of bacteria, yeasts and moulds which oxydise the acids. Thus if soured milk is left for a time, the acidity disappears and the medium becomes suitable for the development of micro-organisms which cause the curd to become putrid and alkaline.

Casein is a protein specific to milk. When precipitated to a curd by lactic acid it can make a soft cheese which is acceptable and tasty but which will not keep. Casein can however, also be precipitated by the action of various enzymes like pepsin and rennin. Rennin is the enzyme which is found naturally in rennet which occurs in the fourth stomach of the calf. When coagulated by rennet, milk undergoes a complex breakdown which is fundamentally different from souring. It is this enzymatic action which continues throughout the cheese-making process which enables cheeses to ripen.

Processes of Cheese-making
There are so many different types of cheese and so many different ways of making them that no one set of steps or processes can apply to all. Many cheeses however, pass through most of these stages.
1. Treatment by heat or ripening of the milk.
2. Renneting the milk to cause coagulation.
3. Cutting the curd.
4. Treatment of the curd in the whey – this can be pitching, or steeping the curd in the whey.
5. Draining off of the whey.
6. Further treatment of curd to expel more whey, e.g. cheddaring or piling curd so that whey is discharged.
7. Milling, i.e. breaking up the curd.
8. Salting the curd.
9. Putting the curd into moulds.
10. Pressing the curd in the mould or in some way consolidating it into a cheese.
11. Ripening the cheese by storing under certain conditions for a set time.

Classification of Cheeses
This is a mammoth subject and one for which no set of rationale has

been expounded. There are accordingly many ways in which cheese can be classified.

Type of Milk
For example, cow's, goat's or sheep. There are, much more rarely, cheeses made from reindeer milk, asses milk and mare's milk.

Type of Coagulation
For example, lactic curd cheeses and rennet curd cheeses.

Consistency
1. Fresh cheeses, those scarcely ripened and soft e.g. fromage frais and cottage cheese.
2. Soft cheeses which although ripened are spreadable e.g. Camembert Limburger.
3. Semi-hard cheeses e.g. Gouda and Stilton. These are firm and smooth but easy to cut.
4. Hard cheeses e.g. Cheddar, Gruyère, Parmesan.

Rind
The various classifications by rind would include: those with no rind, dry rind, white mould rind and red rind.

Fat Content
Classification by fat content is obviously a clear-cut, scientific method.

The Process
There are so many processes that to list them all would be impossible here. However, here are a selection of process-types.
1. Drained cheeses.
2. Moulded but not pressed cheeses.
3. Those with washed or unwashed rind.
4. Cheddared cheeses i.e. those which have undergone the special piling of the curd to expel whey characteristic of the cheddar cheese process.
5. Cooked curd cheeses.
6. Plastic curd or kneaded curd cheeses where the curd is emersed in hot water and kneaded until pliable e.g. Cacciocavallo.
7. Whey cheese can either be the mysost type, where the whey is reduced to a substance the consistency of peanut butter, or the

ricotta type where the milk proteins are flocculated by heating and skimmed as they froth up e.g. Schabzieger.
8. Macerated cheeses. These are steeped to ripen in a liquid, often alcoholic (though not brine).

These are only some of the processes, cheeses also differ in the length of ripening time, the ripening conditions e.g. moist or dry. They can be further categorized of course by size and weight.

EQUIPMENT

With a milk supply and a piece of muslin a simple cottage cheese can be made. If however you want to undertake cheese-making more seriously then there are some pieces of equipment which you will need. Many of them can be improvized and although in this particular art or craft the better the tools the better the results, I will mention any improvisations as I go along. With such makeshift equipment however, one is in a bit of a 'catch twenty-two' situation – one does not want to spend money buying equipment until one knows whether one is going to enjoy cheese-making – and one will not really enjoy it until one achieves good results for which one does need the right equipment.

The Cheese-making Room

The temperature of the cheese room is very important. More people go wrong by confusing the temperature of the dairy which must always be cool, with the temperature of the cheese room which should be in the region of 65-70°F (18-12°C) so that the whey drains successfully from the curd. Two pieces of equipment necessary therefore are a safe room heater which can of course be radiators or hot water pipes. (probably the one advantage of working in the kitchen is that it will be the right sort of temperature anyway) and a room thermometer to ascertain these temperatures. Meshed gauze fitted to the windows will keep fly damage to a minimum.

A Dairy Thermometer

A floating diary thermometer is a very good piece of equipment which will indicate the various temperatures of the milk, curd, whey. This combined with an understanding of the acidity content leads to successful cheese-making.

Acidimeter

While this is not absolutely essential, and the most experienced cheese-maker I know has never used one, for the novice they do take the guesswork out of the process and lead to better results. An acidimeter is really an acidity testing kit. You put 10ccs of the milk or substance to be tested into a special glazed bowl and 3 or 4 drops of phenolphthalein as an indicator. These are stirred and the burette filled by pumping up to the level marked and then the caustic soda dripped into the milk, drop by drop, stirring all the time until the mixture is tinged a permanent pink. Then read off how much caustic soda you have used and that is the acidity level of the sample i.e. the amount of lactic acid is measured by the amount of caustic soda needed to neutralize it.

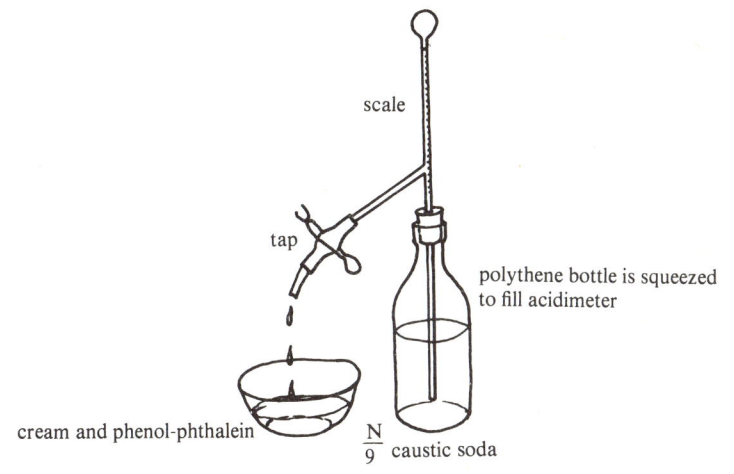

Figure 16. Lloyd's acidimeter

It sounds very difficult written down but is not. If you have not got an acidimeter there are various tests which can help you to determine the acidity at different stages.

The Straw Test

Measure 56 drops of fresh rennet into a warm cup and put in a straw or toothpick and 4 oz. (100g) of milk at 84°F (29°C) noting the time *exactly* with a stop watch or the second hand of a clock. Stir for 15 seconds. Note *exactly* the time the straw stops moving. The shorter the time the milk takes to coagulate the higher the acidity.

Time in Seconds	Percentage Acidity
24	20
21	21
20	22
18	24

Figure 17. Coagulation time indicating milk acidity

Milk at 83°F (25°C) will take 26 seconds to indicate 0.20 per cent acidity. Milk at 85°F (29.5°C) will only take 22 seonds i.e. the result is affected by 2 seconds for every 1°F the milk varies from 84°F (29°C).

The Hot Iron Test
This is used to test the acidity of the curd at pitching time. You need a hot iron or a hot piece of smooth metal. It must not be red hot. Take a piece of the curd and touch it on the hot iron and pull it away. A thin crisp thread will form. This is because of a protein phenomenon. When the lactic acid reacts with the casein salts form, monolactates have the property of becoming fibrous when heated and these 'threads' will pull from it. As the acidity rises however, dilactates form which will not react to heat in this way.

Length of Thread	Percentage Acidity
$\frac{1}{4}''$	0.17
$\frac{1}{2}''$	0.24
$\frac{3}{4}''$	0.45

Figure 18. Length of 'thread' indicating curd acidity

This test has the disadvantage of only being a check on an empirical finding. If the curd is too acid when tested, there is little one can do about it, so obviously it is as well, if using this method, to start testing before you think the right degree of acidity has been reached.

Water Bath

The milk for cheese-making must be heated or cooled slowly and so some sort of water bath, jacketed vat or large double boiler is an essential. In this way hot or cold water can be circulated in the outer container and the milk in the inner pan kept off the direct heat.

A jacketed vat is a large piece of equipment, but has been specifically designed for this purpose.

A Burco boiler is a viable alternative for large quantities.

The boiler can heat water which in turn heats the milk in the churn. The milk in the churn can be cooled either by the use of an in-churn

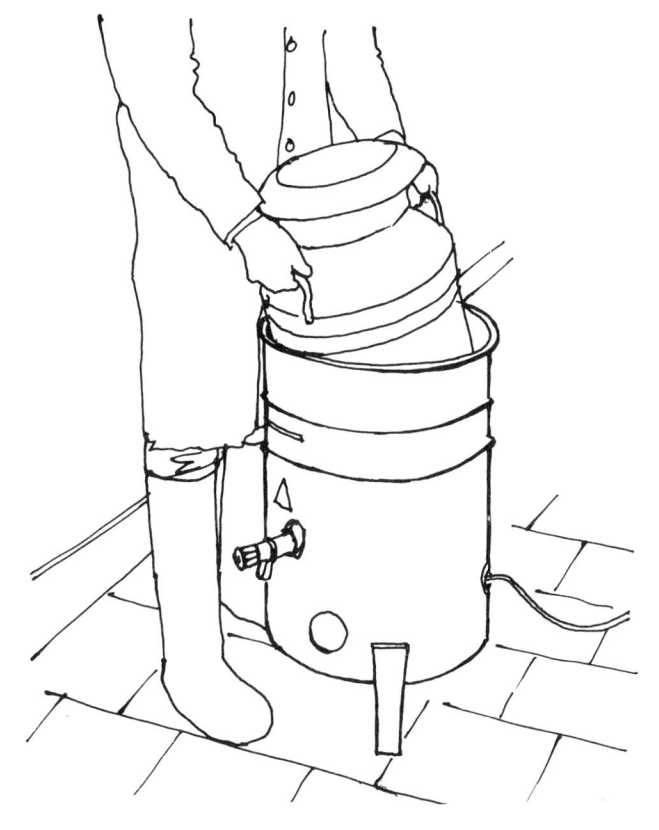

Figure 19. A Burco boiler and churn

cooler or by draining the hot water out of the boiler and circulating cold water in it through a hose pipe.

For smaller amounts there are larger porringers which can be used or a large saucepan standing in a preserving pan.

You can even get away with standing a pan in a sink of hot or cold water and you will certainly appreciate the benefit of low sinks when you have to lift these pans in and out.

If you have none of these you will have to raise the temperature by taking out a saucepanful of whey at a time, warming it and returning it to the whole and stirring it in very gently.

Cheese Presses

You will need a decent press if you want to make good, hard cheese. There are still a few old farm ones available but several excellent new ones have come on the market recently. The Smallholder's Press produced by Self-Sufficiency and Smallholding Supplies is a dual purpose press, useful to cheese-makers and wine-makers. The Wheeler is another good one, well made, efficient and easy to use.

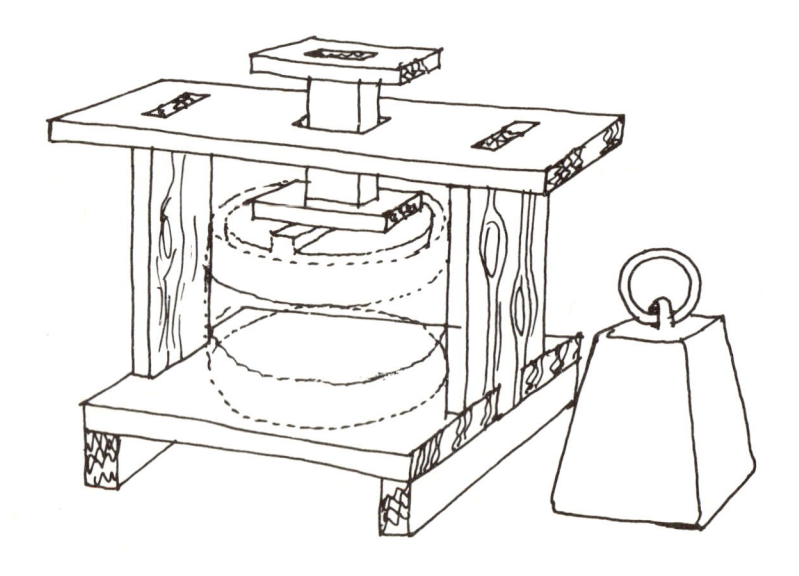

Figure 20. A simple wooden cheese press

A simple wooden press which relies on various weights being placed on top of it is quite easy to make.

CHEESE-MAKING: THE TECHNIQUE 89

There are so many improvisations which can be made, from large stones balanced on coffee tins to adapted book presses. When adapting or constructing something however, be careful that you are not spending as much money as a new one would cost you.

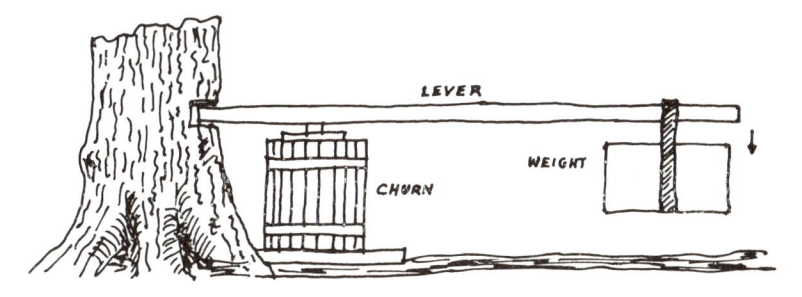

Figure 21. Lever principle cheese press

If you are improvising it is as well to remember that a more even pressure will be achieved by a lever principle than by just pressing down on the top of the cheese. The old diagram of a wooden lever press illustrates this principle perfectly. The pressure is increased by moving the weight along the pole.

Chessit and Follower

The chessit is the cylindrical container in which the cheese is placed to be pressed. It is also referred to as the cheese mould. (This is confusing as the term 'cheese mould' has a second meaning — that of the specific bacteria found in cheese rooms or introduced to cheese to make the individual cheese types). Chessits are normally made with holes through which the whey can drain.

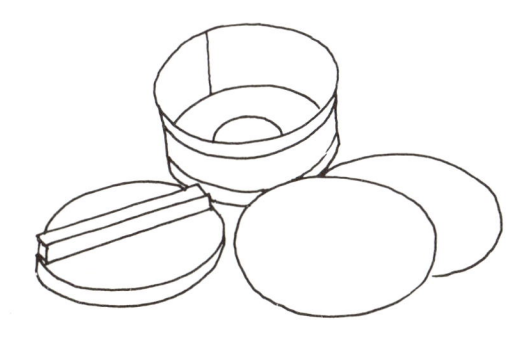

Figure 22. Typical cheese mould with wooden follower and tin discs

The follower is the circle of wood or metal, slightly smaller than the circumference of the chessit which is placed on top of the cheese on which the actual pressure is exerted. It acts as a piston.

There are many good cheese moulds and followers available at the moment and they are very easy to improvise from old coffee tins etc. When you punch holes in home-made moulds, remember that they must be punched from the inside out, otherwise the cheese will be very hard to remove. Never use plastic piping or any material which might contain toxic resins. This applies equally to moulds and draining trays.

Moulds and Draining Trays

For drained rather than pressed cheeses, there are many traditionally shaped moulds. Some are no longer available but many are now being made again. The coulommier mould can be purchased still and there are many sizes of plastic cheese mould available. Improvisation from tins, e.g. cut off square tea tins or round coffee tins are easy to make. Traditionally collars and cane mats were used for draining certain cheeses. Round cane cheese draining mats are now back on the market, hand made in Somerset. They are available from Self-Sufficiency and Smallholding Supplies. There are also plastic draining mats available too; these are guaranteed non-toxic and can be purchased from dairy suppliers. Do not be tempted to use the sort of cane table-mat, imported from the Far-East. These disintegrate if sterilized and also give the cheese a nasty taste and often discolour it.

Trays can be useful to catch the whey from smaller moulds but if you are cheese-making in quantity it is better to equip a bench with guttering and a pipe which will lead the whey directly into a receptacle – never waste it!

A large stockpot type receptacle fitted with a tap is a great boon for draining the whey off stilton type cheese for example. These are obtainable from catering suppliers but can be picked up second-hand.

Curd Cutting Knives

Traditional vertical and horizontal curd cutting knives can sometimes be picked up second-hand but a satisfactory modern equivalent is a length of stainless steel with a right angle bend at one end.

Drawn through the curd it makes columns, which in turn can be made into cubes by immersing the knife in the curd and making circular movements, raising it little by little as you do so.

A large palette knife can be used as an alternative, the result will not be such a neatly cut curd but will not make much difference to the end product.

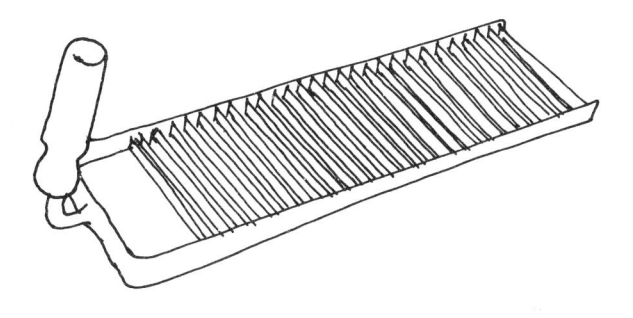

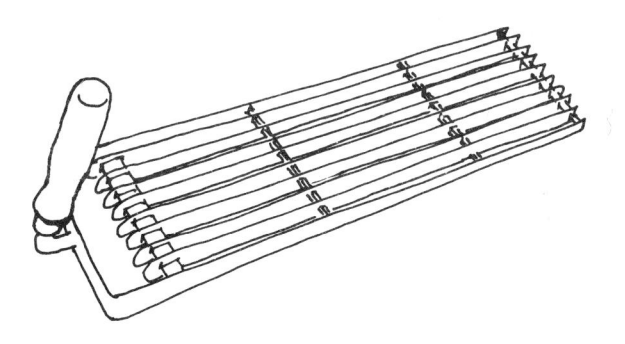

Figure 23. Traditional horizontal and vertical curd knives

You will also need butter muslins and cheese cloths and an assortment of measuring jugs, measuring spoons, ladles, a spoon with perforations or a slice, colanders and scales to weigh the curd for salting. A large table is useful too.

Rennet
Good quality cheese-making rennet is essential for serious cheese-making. Junket rennet will do for some of the soft cheeses. It also incorporates glycerine which inhibits correct ripening but even this loses its strength with age. Rennet can be obtained from many suppliers (see *Useful Addresses*). It must be kept out of the light and is mostly supplied in dark coloured bottles. It should not be shaken as this incorporates air which hastens deterioration. It is obtained from the fourth stomach of a calf by a commercial procedure (no one makes their own any more). It contains the enzymes rennin and pepsin which coagulate the casein in the milk and produce curds and whey and whose enzymatic action continues during the ripening process. Rennet is *always diluted* (with four times its volume of water unless stated differently in a recipe).

Starter
This is a culture of lactic acid-producing bacteria which, when inoculated into milk which has been heat-treated, provides the right start for the cheese-making process. It needs to be propagated for use on a continuing basis and is the single most baffling thing to novices in the whole operation. Really it works on much the same principle as yogurt-making. Milk is heat-treated to remove unwanted bacteria and then inoculated with a strong culture of the bugs one wants which multiply in this their ideal medium.

One is in fact using a stronger and more robust dose of the *naturally* occurring lactic acid producing bacteria which help to produce a firmer curd and a better flavour.

One can make one's own starter but bought cultures ensure better results. They do however need propagating prior to use. To do this some milk must be sterilized to provide the best medium for the starter culture to breed in. You will need some clean bottles (i.e. previously boiled bottles) – these can be either boilable polythene bottles (which have the advantage that they can be deep-frozen), tonic water bottles or baby's orange juice bottles. Fill the bottles to the neck with milk, screw on the caps and then unscrew them a little and either:

1. Pressure cook them for 10 minutes at 15 lbs pressure, placing a

CHEESE-MAKING: THE TECHNIQUE 93

mat of some sort or a wooden trivet in the bottom of the cooker so that the bottles are not touching the base or
2. Place them on similar trivet in a deep pan and fill with water to level of necks and boil for two hours.

Cool the bottles naturally and tighten the caps. You now have several bottles of sterile milk, which will keep in the fridge for a week.

Inoculating the Milk with the Starter Culture
You now want to get the culture into the milk without allowing any other bacteria to enter as well.

If you want to be sure of this, the best method is to use Lewis bottles, these are polythene bottles with rubber seals. The culture is transferred from one bottle to another by using a double ended hollow needle, this pierces through the rubber seal and by gentle pressure on the bottle, the culture passes inside the needle from one bottle to the other without ever coming in contact with air.

Figure 24. Transferring the starter culture

This is a good method for perfectionists but the same result can be obtained by inoculating the culture over boiling water or a flame. This will temporarily displace any airborne bacteria. Shake your starter and loosen the cap of one of your bottles. Working above the pan of boiling water or the flame (and taking care not to get burned) quickly transfer a teaspoonful of the starter into the bottle of sterile milk and seal quickly. If you are using polythene bottles they can be deep-frozen. Otherwise the newly inoculated bottle must be incubated prior to use.

Incubation
For the culture to develop successfully it must be kept at a temperature of 70°F (21°C) for 8-12 hours. An airing cupboard is adequate for this or an egg incubator set low. A good incubator can be made from a wooden box fitted with a light bulb. This is especially useful if you have nowhere to incubate yogurt, as the same box with a higher wattage light bulb will serve this purpose. For one bottle a baby's bottle warmer makes a good incubator.

The consistency of the incubated starter should be like runny yogurt. It can then be placed in the fridge until used.

Suggested Programme for Continuing Use
1. If you invest in polythene bottles and have a deep-freeze, this is much simpler. Just inoculate as many bottles as you have, and incubate one for immediate cheese-making and deep-freeze the others, bring them out one by one and incubate just prior to use.
2. If glass bottles are used, inoculate two bottles, one for immediate use and one to be placed in the fridge where it will last a week. Incubate this and at the same time re-cultivate a further two bottles. The samples should remain good like this but if the culture appears to separate then it is a sign that the lactic acid producing bacteria have used up all the food in the milk and are beginning to perish. Immediate re-propagation can save the culture but if the starter does not give a firm set within 12 hours it should be thrown away and a new culture bought.

Making Your Own Starter
This will not be as effective as using a bought one but in summer there is no reason why you should not try it. Take half a gallon (2.2 litres) of fresh, clean milk (not foremilk) and keep this in a bowl in a clean dairy at a temperature of 70°-75°F (21°-24°C). Let it curdle.

When it has curdled take some freshly milked milk and run it through a separator (you do not want the cream). Pasteurize this. Skim the top off the curdled milk (removing cream) and stir the rest into the cooled pasteurized milk. You have thus inoculated sterile milk with a culture of lactic acid producing bacteria. Cover and incubate at 70°-75°F (21°-24°C) for 24 hours. Skim off any cream. Use what remains as a starter.

This method uses the bacteria from your own dairy and is the basis on which traditional dairies worked prior to the isolation of cultures. The more cheese that has been made in a particular dairy the more cheese bugs there will be in the atmosphere. These give originality and flavour and were the basis of all regional cheeses.

If you are attempting to reproduce a cheese a tiny bit of shop-bought cheese crumbled in with the starter does help to ensure that some of the right bugs are present.

Lastly if you have not got any starter, try using a little cultured buttermilk. It is not as good but helps to speed up the coagulation process.

Annatto
This is the only colouring agent you should use for cheese. Other food colourings give strange results. Annatto is obtainable from dairy suppliers. (see *Useful Addresses*.)

Wax
As an alternative to bandaging some cheeses you finish them with a coating of paraffin wax. This can be clear, or can be coloured red or black. Put pieces of wax in a double saucepan with a wide enough neck to be able to dip the cheese in. Melt wax slowly, stirring it from time to time. Deep cheese rotating it to ensure that every part is covered. Cheese wax can be made from melted down candle stubs or can be purchased from dairy suppliers. I have never tried it, but cannot see why beeswax would not make a good coat for cheese.

Records
It is interesting to note down every step in the cheese-making process. This is a great help in tracing any faults as well as enabling you to reproduce your successes! Special cheese record books can be obtained from the suppliers but of course you can keep a notebook yourself noting quantities, temperatures, and durations of the different stages.

7
CHEESE-MAKING RECIPES

The easiest way to learn the cheese-making technique is slowly, as one goes along, by actually making different cheeses. If one starts with easier cheeses and progresses to more difficult ones, a lot of the mystique disappears and ones confidence increases so that the harder cheeses become a pleasant challenge rather than disaster areas.

To illustrate basic cheese-making techniques I propose to deal in detail with the making of four cheeses:
1. A Cottage cheese
2. A simple unpressed Coulommier type cheese
3. A semi-soft cheese of the Stilton type
4. A pressed cheese using the cheddaring process, often called smallholder's cheese.

Cleanliness
At the risk of repeating this many times, I will stress once again that all the equipment which comes into contact with milk or cheese must be sterilized or it will inoculate unwanted bacteria into the product.

1. Cottage Cheese
This is the simplest type of cheese to make. Take some separated or skimmed milk (more than 2 pints or a litre – less is hardly worthwhile) and curdle it by adding starter, sour milk or buttermilk or even some yogurt. Leave in a warm place for 24 hours. Heat very gently in a double pan to separate curd from whey. Strain curd gently into a sterile cloth over a colander and drain.
Scrape down from sides of muslin and drain again. When fully drained, salt to taste and eat at once. Herbs can be chopped and added for variety.

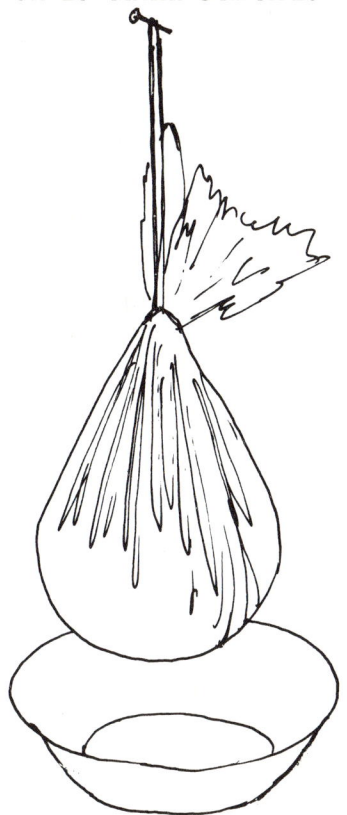

Figure 25. Draining the curd

2. Coulommier Cheese
From this it is an easy step to make a Coulommier cheese which introduces us to rennet and starter.

Materials
1 gallon milk (4.5 litres)
Starter
Rennet
Salt
Large water bath pan i.e. double saucepan or porringer
Coulommier moulds (these are in pairs which fit one on top of the

98   MAKING CHEESES, BUTTERS, CREAM AND YOGURT

other. This amount will make 4 cheese so you need 4 pairs of moulds.)
Draining mats
Saucers

Raise the temperature of the milk to 158°F (70°C) and cool immediately to 90°F (32.2°C) using water bath. Add 1 tablespoonful of starter and stir well. Leave for 30 minutes to ripen. Add rennet, 1 teaspoonful diluted in 4 times its own volume of water.

Stir only until stir marks appear on the curd. Leave undisturbed in warm atmosphere for 1-1½ hours until curd is firm.

While curd is firming set up the moulds in pairs over a draining tray. Make sure they are steady as when full they can become top heavy and tip.

Figure 26. Coulommier mould in position on straw mat

Test curd by placing the back of your hand against it; it should come away without leaving a milk film.

Using the top of one of the moulds, cut four perfect circles out of the curd, leave them on saucers. These are to make neat tops for your cheeses. Then using a perforated spoon or slice, cut slices thinly from the curd and fill each mould bit by bit. By filling each mould little by little rather than one at a time the whey runs evenly from them all. When they are almost full, take the saucers and carefully slide the 'tops' on to each cheese.

The curd will sink as the whey continues to drain and by the next day will be below the top mould or hoop. Remove these and put a draining mat over the top of each cheese and a rack on top and invert the cheeses carefully. Repeat this turning a second time the next day.

The cheeses will have then shrunk from the moulds and the moulds can be removed. Do not attempt to unmould too soon. Sprinkle salt on the tops and bottoms of the cheeses and rub gently in.

This cheese can be eaten immediately or kept for a week but it has a tendency to dry out.

If a salty cheese is liked omit the salting and keep in brine for 2 weeks.

3. Stilton Type Cheese

Making this cheese teaches one quite a bit about acidity, which some people find hard to grasp. The making of Stilton type cheese (one must not call it Stilton proper as this is the perogative of the members of the Stilton Cheese-makers Association who have certificates of authorization) is not however, difficult but the subsequent looking after the cheese is a bit hazardous.

Materials
3 gallons (13.6 litres) of milk. (This is not heat-treated and so must be of the best and freshest quality.)
1 teaspoonful of diluted rennet
1 or 2 large pans
Thermometer
Knife
Cheese cloth
Colander
Salt
A 'stilton' mould

Heat the milk to 85°F (29°C) and rennet. Stir very gently and leave for 1 hour. Cut curd in slices and ladle into cloth placed over colander. Fold over the edges of the cloth and leave curd steeping in whey for 2 hours or until the acidity reaches 0.125 per cent. The ambient temperature is of importance as warmth helps even acidity to develop and the curd should not become chilled throughout this process. If you are using goats milk the acidity develops very slowly and the process may take as long as two days. Tie the cloth in a stilton knot i.e. take the corners and wind one around the other three very firmly. Pour off some of the whey. In 2-3 hours tighten bundle and pour off more whey. Repeat until whey shows acidity of 0.17 per cent.

When the acidity reaches 0.2 per cent the curd should be turned out of the cloth. It should be firm not spongey. (It should sound like a baby's bottom when smacked!) It may be left until 0.5 per cent acidity is reached. (Hot iron test of $\frac{1}{4}$ inch threads.)

Mill the curd into walnut sized pieces and about 1 oz. (25g) of salt should be added. Have ready a mould standing on a mat. This mould is used unlined. Back the curd tightly into the mould, lining the sides and bottom of the mould with smaller pieces and the centre as far as possible with larger pieces. Do not press. Leave in temperature of 70°F (21°C) for about a week to drain. Turn daily. It will shrink from the mould by the end of the week and smell of ripe pears.

You must now encourage the cheese to develop a good 'coat' by scraping and filling any crevices with the scrapings. Bandage firmly but not too tightly (you can put the cheese back in the mould if you like). Each day remove bandage, scrape and re-bandage. Do this daily until the cheese has developed a good coat with a white powdery outside. This is not quick or easy – the cheese goes through some very smelly stages. Once the white mould has developed the cheese can be freed from its bandages and ripened at 55°F (13°C) for about a month. Turn twice a week and brush to keep cheese mites off. Should be mature in four months.

Some people pierce the cheese with stainless steel needles to encourage blueing by admitting air which they hope will contain the right bugs. Sometimes blueing develops spontaneously when the cheese is cut. The taste and texture are of a 'blue' cheese anyway.

4. Smallholder's Cheese
A semi-hard cheese which sets out clearly more of the basic cheese-making procedures.

Materials
2 gallons (9 litres) of milk.
Starter
Rennet
Large pan
Thermometer
Slice
Palette knife
Curd knife
Cheese cloths, one for 'cheddaring' one for lining the mould
Mould and follower
Press
Bandages

Heat the milk to 155°F (68°C) and cool to 90°F (32°C). Add 2 tablespoonsful of starter. Stir well and leave for 30 minutes then rennet using 1 teaspoonful of rennet diluted with 6 teaspoonsful of water. Stir until stir marks appear. If using cow's milk top stir to prevent the cream rising. If this cheese is to be rich the cream must be evenly dispersed throughout. Leave to set until curd splits cleanly over your finger.

To the curd, first loosen it from the sides of the pan with the palette knife, then cut into inch cubes, either by using curd knife or improvising with a long scalded knife.

Leave to settle for a few minutes while you wash your hand and forearm thoroughly. Then scald the curd, i.e. put the pan on a very gentle heat and slowly heat curd to 110-106°F (46-41°C) gently moving the curd with your hand to prevent one part's heating more than another and to stop lumps from forming. This will take about 20-30 minutes.

Next pitch i.e leave the curd in the whey to develop acidity. Leave for 30 minutes. The curd is now quite different, yellow in colour and of a 'marshmallowy' texture.

Then drain the whey. It can either be ladled off or a cloth placed over another pan and it tipped in. Form the curd into a bundle in cloth on tray tipped slightly so that whey continues to drain for 20 minutes. Then cheddar i.e. cut the curd into 4 thick slices, re-tie and drain for another 20 minutes and then open bundle and cut the slices into 8, re-stack them and tie and drain. After another 20 minutes untie the bundle and restack the pieces in a different order. Repeat until firm and of 'chicken breast' texture.

Then mill i.e. break up the curd into nut-size pieces, these should 'squeak' as you touch them. They look a bit like scrambled egg. Salt at the rate of $\frac{1}{2}$ oz. (6g) salt to 1 lb (450g) of curd. Mould by lining the mould with sterile cloth and pressing the curd evenly into it. Cover the top with a corner of the cloth, avoiding thick creases, and put on the follower. Press at 7 lbs (3kg) weight for 2 hours, increase to 28 lbs (13kg) and leave overnight. The next day take out of mould, take cloth off, turn cheese, put in a clean sterile muslin and put back. Increase pressure to 56 lbs (25.5kg). Repeat for 2 more days. Then take out of mould and if there are no cracks dip it into water of 150°F (66°C) for 30 seconds. This helps form rind. Return to 56 lbs (25.5kg) pressure. Repeat this turning and re-wrapping the cheese for a few more days until it feels firm. If there is any suggestion of springiness keep applying the pressure – you can go up to 112 lbs (50.5kg).

MAKING CHEESES, BUTTERS, CREAM AND YOGURT

Remove from press and leave in a cool room protected from flies for a few hours to dry out. Then either wax or bandage the cheese. To bandage, cut 2 circles from the butter muslin $\frac{1}{2}$ in. (1cm) larger than the top and bottom of the cheese and a band $\frac{1}{2}$ in. (1cm) deeper. Use lard to smooth and press the bandage on, try to make sure there are no creases. Traditionally these bandages were sewn in place by lock-stitch.

A special cheese paste, Edifas, is used commercially. It is particularly good as it contains a fly deterrent and is easy to use being something of the consistency of wall-paper glue. It is only available at the moment in large quantities which is a pity. Perhaps a distributor will take the hint!

After this ripen by storing on an airy shelf at 50°-60°F (10°-16°C) turning frequently. The ripening room should be this bit cooler than the cheese-making room. A special room is not necessary, you can suspend the cheese in a string bag from anywhere clean in the house where the temperature is right.

It is ready in 3-4 weeks but should keep much longer.

What Went Wrong?

Failure to Coagulate
This can be because of residue of the sterilizing solution (if you have been using hypochlorite type) has infiltrated the milk. The rennet may be too old or too weak or the milk may come from a cow which is on antibiotics.

Tests for Coagulation
If you are not sure whether milk has coagulated float a straw or toothpick on it – when it stops moving stop stirring or you will release too much whey.

You can also test by seeing if curd splits cleanly over your finger.

Alternatively, drip a little water onto the curd, if it stays there coagulation has been achieved, if it is absorbed, leave longer to complete coagulation.

Failure to Ripen
This can be caused by the sterilizing solution too, especially in the cheese cloth which should therefore always be boiled.

Cheese Fly
This is a fly which lays its eggs in the cracks in cheese. After about 3 days the eggs hatch and the larvae eat their way through the cheese until they become adults. They are known as 'jumpers' because of their rapid movement.

House Fly
This is the bluebottle and it produces eggs which turn into very unpleasant maggots.

Cheese Mite
This is a member of the spider family and is very tiny. It burrows extensively into cheese throughout its complex life cycle and causes a lot of damage.

Temperature and Humidity
Cheese which burst on you or dry into a pile of acid crumbs or disintegrate into a slimy mess are very disappointing. Probably the temperature and humidity of the ripening room are at fault although no doubt the acidity levels were wrong somewhere along the line.

Yeasts
The idea of a dual purpose wine and cheese press is excellent but a great deal of care has to be taken that the yeasts connected with wine-making (or indeed bread-making) do not gain access to your cheese because they will inhibit the action of the enzymes in ripening the cheese.

Traditional Cheeses
You will wish to experiment with other types of cheese and I am including some traditional British cheeses here for that purpose. Remember that you cannot reproduce exactly the conditions which have made these cheeses what they are. You can however learn something from each of them which will help you to find 'your' cheese, the cheese you find satisfying to make, which your family enjoy and which encapsulates something of your own farm or smallholding. If this could only happen throughout the British Isles we would really see a revival of the old tradition of farmhouse cheeses.

Caerphilly

Leave night's milk standing overnight and skim cream off in morning. Heat the cream to 90°F (32°C) and add back to the milk. Then add morning's milking.

Heat to 70°F (21°C). Add starter, 3 tablespoonsful for every 2 gallons (9 litres). Continue to raise temperature gently to 86°F (30°C). Add rennet using 1 teaspoonful of diluted rennet for each 2 gallons (9 litres). Top stir until coagulation begins (i.e. stir marks occur). Cover and leave for 40 minutes.

Cut curd in 1 in. (2.5cm) cubes and stir gently with hand for 20 minutes. Raise temperature to 89°F (31°C) and when acidity reaches 16 per cent drain the whey and mill the curd into walnut sized pieces. Salt, using $\frac{1}{2}$ teaspoonful per 1 lb (450g) and ladle into cloth lined mould. Press for 10 minutes at 4 lbs (1.8kg), turn and repeat twice. Leave overnight. It can be immersed in a brine bath for 24 hours, then drained. Ripen for 10 days.

Cheshire

Leave evenings milk to stand overnight and in the morning skim the cream, warm it and return it to whole (as for last recipe) and then mix with morning's meal.

Heat to 120°F (49°C) and cool to 90°F (32°C). When acidity reaches 0.2 per cent add starter, 3 tablespoonsful per 2 gallons (9 litres). Heat to 84°F (29°C) and rennet with 1 teaspoonful diluted with water. Stir for 10 minutes, top stirring to disperse cream. Leave to coagulate.

Cut curd into 1 in. (2.5cm) cubes, handling very carefully to keep fat intact in curd. Leave for 5 minutes then gradually heat to 93°F (34°C) stirring with hand all the time.

Pitch for 40 minutes then drain whey and cheddar when firm. Mill curd into tiny pieces and salt fairly heavily i.e. 1 teaspoonful to 1 lb (450g).

Put into moulds lined with muslin and keep in a warm place. The next day change cloth and press, beginning lightly and increasing pressure over three days. Turn daily. Then remove cloth take out cheese and bandage. Ripen at 55°-60°F (13°-16°C) turning frequently, for about 3 months.

Colby

Warm some milk to 90°F (32°C) add 1 teaspoonful of starter per gallon (4.5 litres). Leave overnight. In the morning heat to 80°F (27°C) and rennet using 1 teaspoonful of diluted rennet per gallon (4.5 litres) Leave to coagulate. Cut curd carefully, stirring lightly. Heat to 100°F (38°C) to contract curd further, hand stirring all the time. Turn off heat and pitch for another half an hour or so.

Then drain whey, hang the curd up in a cheesecloth and drain for another hour. Add salt to curd to taste. Put into fresh cloth in mould.

Press for 2 days gradually increasing pressure. Turn daily. Ripen for a few days. It is then ready to eat.

Colwick

This is a soft cheese traditionally made with a dished top which can be filled with cream.

Heat milk to 155°F (68°C) and cool to 90°F (32°C). Rennet using 1 teaspoonful of diluted rennet per gallon (4.5 litres). Add 1 tablespoonful of starter at the same time. Top stir for 10 minutes and then cover and leave for 40 minutes.

Line the moulds (traditionally, in a round mould 5 in. (13cm) in diameter and about 7 in. (18.5cm) high a gallon of milk will make two such cheeses) with cloths large enough to fold over the tops of the curd. Cut neat 'tops' as for Coulommier cheese and keep them on saucers. Fill moulds with thin slices of curd and finish with the tops. Leave to drain for an hour. Then pull muslin upwards so that curd is pulled away from the sides of the mould. This produces the characteristic dished shape. The cheese is therefore *not* turned.

Allow to drain for 35 hours in a warm temperature. Remove muslin carefully. It is not salted as it is a sweet cheese to eat filled with whipped cream. Can be eaten at once.

Cotherstone

Set evenings milk and in the morning skim cream, heat it and return it together with morning's meal.

Heat to 70°F (21°C) and add starter using 1 tablespoonful to 2 gallons (9 litres) and continue to heat until temperature reaches 80°F (27°C). Measure acidity and when it reaches approximately 0.19 per cent add rennet using ½ teaspoonful of diluted rennet for 2 gallons (9 litres). This type of cheese must not work too quickly. Stir and when stir marks appear cover and leave for an hour.

Cut curd into cubes (handling very gently as the curd is so soft) and bring temperature slowly up to 86°F (30°C) stirring gently.

Pitch until acidity reaches 0.14 per cent then drain whey. Cut the curd into large cubes and then mill and salt. Salt using ¼ oz. (6g) to 1 lb (450g) of curd. Pack the curd very lightly into lined moulds and leave to settle and drain for 2 hours. Press overnight or longer if cheese is large, remove and bandage. Turn daily and ripen for about two weeks in a moist, draught-free atmosphere.

Crowdie
Heat one gallon (4.5 litres) of separated milk (skim milk) to 155°F (68°C) to 90°F (32°C). Stir in 1 tablespoonful of starter. Leave for 10 minutes and rennet with 1 teaspoonful of diluted rennet. Stir until stir marks appear. Leave for 2 hours or until firm, test with back of hand. Cut curd into 1 inch (2.5cm) cubes.

Raise temperature to 100°F (38°C) stirring all the time. This should be done over 20 minutes then pitch for another 10 minutes. Ladle the curd into a muslin and drain in a warm place. Remove from muslin and salt to taste. Pat into shapes. This can be eaten immediately but will deep-freeze well. It is a cheese from Scotland, traditionally eaten with oatcakes.

Derby
Mix morning's milk with previous evening's and heat to 84°F (29°C). Add rennet and stir. Leave for 45 minutes then cut curd into cubes. Bring temperature up to 94°F (34°C) stirring with hand all the time then pitch for 30 minutes. Then drain whey, cut curd and cheddar for 30 minutes. Mill and salt using ¼ oz. (6g) to 1 lb (450g) of curd.

Press lightly in lined moulds. Gradually increase pressure over 4 hours. Leave at maximum pressure for next day. Turn, replace in clean cloth. Do this for 2 more days. Rinse in a light brine and ripen for a month.

Cheddar
This is a whole milk cheese and one of the best. Test acidity of evening's milk. Leave evening's milk to stand overnight and in morning skim cream. Heat the cream and return to milk. Then add morning's milk. Heat to 85°F (21°C) and the acidity should be about 0.02 per cent above that of the previous evening. Rennet with diluted rennet (1 teaspoonful to 2 gallons or 9 litres). Stir for about 10 minutes or until it coagulates. It is ready for cutting when the curd splits cleanly over the fingers. Then cut curd into 2 in. (5cm) cubes with

curd knife. (Traditionally it was then broken further with a curd breaker.) Raise the temperature to 100°F (38°C) very slowly. Then pitch the curd. It should sink to the bottom and be 'hard and shotty'. Leave until whey reaches acidity of 0.19 per cent. Then drain whey and cheddar and then mill and salt using 1 oz. (25g) to 3 lbs (1.3kg) of curd.

Place curd in lined moulds and press gently at first increasing to maximum over 24 hours. Turn, place in clean cloth. Repeat this for 4 days. Remove from mould and bandage. Ripen at 65°F (18°C) for 6 weeks. Turn daily. Then remove to cooler room 55°-60°F (13°-16°C) and turn on alternate days for another 6 weeks.

Double Gloucesters
Traditionally made from the morning's meal. This cheese can be coloured by the addition of annatto. Warm the milk to 85°F (29°C). Rennet (1 teaspoonful of diluted rennet to 1 gallon or 4.5 litres of milk). When the curd sets, skim and press the curd and removing completely from whey cut curd into cubes. Place in a sieve or in a lined mould with a top and place a weight on top. Leave in warm place to encourage whey to drain and when it stops draining cut the curd into smaller cubes and keep in warmth for a further 20 minutes. Then mill and salt very lightly.

Place in cloth-lined moulds and press (turning daily) at moderate pressure, increasing gradually. When cloth is quite dry remove from press and bandage. Ripen turning daily.

Leicester
This is a russet coloured cheese of flaky texture.

Add morning's milk to evening's and heat to 85°F (29°C). Add starter at rate of 1 tablespoonful per 2 gallons (9 litres) and add annatto too. Rennet and leave for an hour. Cut curd very small and heat to 94°F (34°C) stirring very slowly but frequently. Drain off the whey and cheddar. Then mill and salt using 1 oz. (25g) to 3 lbs (1.3kg) of curd.

Put in lined mould and press gently at first increasing gradually. After 12 hours turn and leave for 24 hours under maximum pressure. Bandage and ripen, turning daily, for 3 months.

Shropshire Sage
This is a whole milk cheese.

Heat milk to 155°F (68°C) cool to 90°F (32°C) stir in starter, adding 1 tablespoonful to 1 gallon (4.5 litres). Rennet and stir until stir marks appear. If using cow's milk top stir. Leave to coagulate then cut curd into ½ in. (1cm) cubes and heat gently to 100-110°F (38-43°C). Pitch for 20 minutes, then drain whey. Then cheddar, mill and salt, allowing ½ oz. (12g) to 1 lb (450g) of curd. At the same time add 1 oz. (25g) of sage.

Fill moulds and press at 14-28 lbs (6.5-13kg) pressure. Turn, re-wrap and re-press at 56 lbs (25.5kg) pressure. The next day repeat. When the cheese is firm suspend it in cloth in water at a temperature of 150°F (65°C) for 30 seconds to firm rind then re-wrap and press at full pressure. Continue for four more days. Bandage and ripen for 3 months.

Wensleydale
A soft flaky cheese.

Leave the evening's milk to stand (making sure that it is cooled or excess acidity will develop). In the morning skim the cream, heat it to 90°F (32°C) and add morning's milk. Add starter, allowing ½ tablespoonful for 1 gallon (4.5 litres). Heat all to 84°F (29°C) and when acidity reaches 0.19 per cent rennet, allowing 1 teaspoonful (diluted) for 1 gallon (4.5 litres). Stir until stir marks appear then cut curd carefully. Like Cotherstone this is a slow working cheese and you do not want the curd particles to drain too quickly. Leave curd at bottom of vat to settle for 20 minutes, then stirring very gently heat to 85°F (29.5°C). When the whey shows acid level of 0.14 per cent, pitch for an hour, then drain whey very carefully, pulling all the curd gently to the side of the vessel and drawing off the whey (a vat with a tap is ideal here). Place curd in cloths and pull up corners to make bundles, leave to drain on racks or sloping boards for 20 minutes. Untie and cut curds. Tie up again and continue this process until the curd shows acidity of 0.28 per cent. This should take 45 minutes to 1 hour. Take care that the curd does not chill as this checks development and makes for a weak or badly flavoured cheese. Then mill the curd and salt using ¼ oz. (6g) of salt to 1 lb (450g) of curd.

Place loosely in unlined moulds, packing smaller pieces of curd at top and bottom to make an even surface. Leave to drain for 3 hours then remove, put in cloth and put back in mould overnight. Make sure the temperature is constant at about 65°F (18°C). Turn the cheese and the next day press at 56 lbs (25.5kg) for about 2 hours. It is then removed and bandaged and then put back under pressure again. Ripening takes place in a lowish moist atmosphere as in a cellar. Sometimes the cheeses are ripened in a stilton hoop to make sure they do not become misshapen. Turn daily for first 6 weeks and then on alternate days until ready – about six months in all.

York or Cambridge Cheese
Traditionally they are made in a rectangular mould, like a tall bread, baking tin. It was placed on a straw mat and had an orange stripe. They are known as York or Cambridge because they were sold in markets around Ely as well as all over Yorkshire.

$1\frac{1}{2}$ gallons (7 litres) makes 2 cheeses. Heat milk to 155°F (68°C) cool to 90°F (32°C) and add 1 teaspoonful of starter. Add 1 teaspoonful of diluted rennet. Stir well for 1 minute and then remove 4 pints (2 litres) for the stripe. To this add 1 teaspoonful of annatto and stir until blended.

Do not top stir as this cheese should have creamy tops. Cover both containers and leave for an hour. Cut tops and leave on saucers, as in making Coulommier cheese. Ladle thin slices of curd into the moulds until just over a third full. Divide the orange curd between the moulds and then finish with the rest of the white curd and finally slip the creamy tops into place. Leave to drain for 2-3 days. Do not turn. When firm enough, remove moulds and the cheeses are ready. They were always cut in three to show the stripe and the cream.

Foreign Cheese
There are about a thousand types of cheese marketed from all over the world, many of them available in England. There are specialist shops like Paxton & Whitfield in Jermyn Street in London which not only stock an enormous variety but store them correctly and sell them at the correct ripeness. Even the most modest supermarket stocks *some* foreign cheese and even if they are not well ripened or have suffered from heavy refrigeration you can still be lucky and find a good cheese which has survived.

Most of these cheeses will now have been made in large creameries in their countries of origin but France at least still has a thriving trade in *fermier* cheese made in the regions on farms from unpasteurized milk and commanding a higher price than the similar *laitier* or creamery product.

Adapting Ideas
So there are opportunities for the enthusiast to sample some of the world's best cheeses. As a home dairyer, some of them will fascinate you and you will wish to emulate them. With your increased knowledge of the principles and procedures you will probably be able to arrive at an approximation of the original but do not be disappointed because you will never be able to achieve in your home cheese room the result achieved by generations of cheese-makers in a Swiss valley or Greek hillside. What you can do is to adapt the ideas given to you by other cheeses: after all the famous Tilsit cheese only came into being because a woman in Tilsit in the nineteenth century made a Gouda which she stored in a too-damp cellar, it went soft and cracked and a new cheese was born.

In the same way it is interesting to try some of the foreign cheese processes; for example, maceration, plasticity or smoking.

However if you can, take a trip to a good cheese merchant occasionally and sample the fruits of someone else's labours. In this way you can learn a lot. You can also use a fragment of a bought cheese to add to your own starter when trying to reproduce a special cheese flavour. This may not work exactly but does ensure that some of the right bugs are present.

It is quite impossible to choose from all the hundreds of cheeses in order to give recipes here. My selection is quite random and there are many many others I could have included. One thing about cheese-making, it does lend a different dimension to your travels. If you carry a notebook and visit local cheese-makers you will have edible memories of your holidays on your table.

Port-du-Salut
Once again one should affix the word 'type' to all the following, as these names are usually under licence to the region's cheese-makers only. The real Port-du-Salut is made by the Trappist monks at Entrammes. When these monks returned after being exiled in the reign of Napoleon they brought a dozen dairy cows with them and developed the art of making this flat cylindrical cheese with its yellow rind. To make a sort of Port-du-Salut firstly heat milk to 90°F (32°C) and rennet. Stir deeply for 3-4 minutes, then top stir. Leave until it has coagulated and then cut curd into ½-inch (1cm) cubes. Stir and raise temperature to 106°F (41°C) keeping curd moving slowly. When it is tough and bright turn off heat and pitch for 15 minutes. Drain whey, mill, salt and pack into moulds lined with cheesecloth. Press at 56 lbs

(25.5kg) pressure. Turn and return to press. After 12 hours take out and bandage, return to press for one hour and then ripen for 3 weeks.

Pont L'Evêque

This is a Normandy cheese from the Pays d'Auge. It is a small yellow washed cheese similar in type to the Camembert.

Prepare several small moulds, lining with cloths and placing them on draining trays. Heat milk to 90°F (32°C). Add rennet, cover pan to retain heat and leave for 30 minutes to form soft curd. Cut curd into 1 in. (2.5cm) cubes. Leave to settle for 5 minutes and then using slice cut thin slices of curd and fill moulds. Work fairly swiftly and when all the curd is in the moulds, fold the cloth over to form a flat bundle, take out of mould and take a cloth (using tongs) which you have wrung out in boiling water and place this cloth over the flat bundle. This helps the whey to drain quickly and this is essential for the flavour of this cheese.

After 20 minutes open the bundle and cut the curd into 1 in. (2.5cm) cubes to drain more. Then break up the curd by hand and pack into the unlined moulds which should be on the draining mat. When you have half packed the mould sprinkle a thick layer of salt. Fill completely and place another mat on top. Turn over. Turn every few hours on the first day and then turn daily.

After 4 days you will find they have shrunk and moulds can be removed. Continue to turn for a couple more days when they can either be eaten or ripened, still turning daily, until a mould appears. Wrap in waxed paper and stack. They should then have a rind but be soft inside.

Fromage Blanc

I am particularly fond of the French curd cheeses which are known as fromage blanc or fromage frais. Often these are just eaten with an assortment of jams and the contrasting acid curd and sweet jam is quite delicious.

Coeur à la Crème is a lovely variation. This is made by mixing 8 oz. (225g) of cottage or acid curd cheese with 2 oz. (50g) sugar and $\frac{1}{4}$ pint (150ml) of double cream. Then whisk 2 egg whites until stiff and fold them into the mixture. Spoon the mixture into the same heart shaped moulds as used in crémets d'Angers or little wicker baskets, lined with muslin. Then chill. When firm take out of muslin and serve with jams, or just whipped cream.

Crema di Mascherpone

This is an Italian sweet cream cheese. It has many uses, and can be salted, eaten with fruit or made into a delicious sweet by beating in sugar and liqueur. It is another borderline case, being something between a real cheese and fermented cream.

A pint (550ml) of double cream, left to go thick and drained in a muslin (it must of course be *unpasteurized* cream) with castor sugar and a little kirsch beaten in, gives something of the authentic taste.

Neufchâtel

These lovely cheeses from the Pays du Bray, not far from Dieppe were imported into England as early as the fifteenth century. They are soft paste cheeses of a light refreshing flavour. There are several types, the best known is Bondon which is cylindrically shaped but there are also carrés, briquettes and coeurs.

In the evening heat milk to 120°F (49°C) and cool to 65°F (18°C). Add starter and a little rennet (about half normal amount). Leave overnight. Next morning cut the curd and leave all day in whey. In evening drain whey and hang curd in a cloth. Next morning take down, salt using ½ oz. (12g) to 2 lbs (900g) of curd, work well in and pat into shape with scotch hands.

Ewe's Cheese

There are many Mediterranean sheep milk cheeses. Often they contain recipes not only for a curd cheese but also for a whey cheese. This was born of necessity, as in these poor lands nothing was wasted. The milk of the Sopravissina ewes in Italy is used to make Pecorino which varies from district to district but is based on the same method. The whey produced as a by-product of the Pecorino is used to make the Ricotta (or re-cooked) cheese.

In Greece and the Middle East similar cheeses known as Halloumi (the curd cheese) and Anari (the whey cheese) are made. Both these cheeses are made using wicker baskets instead of moulds.

Halloumi

Heat milk and rennet at 96°F (35°C). Leave for half an hour and test with hand. If curd has formed break it up with your hand and then put on gentle heat while you prepare the baskets. Take off heat and drain whey keeping it clean as it is used for the anari. Take handfuls of curd and squeeze to about the size of golf balls. Pack into the wicker basket, pressing lightly until basket is full. While it drains make the Anari.

Anari
Heat the whey to 185°F (85°C) and add about 25 per cent fresh milk (ewe's or goat's). Stir lightly. Soon the albumin, helped by the casein in the fresh milk, will begin to flocculate and appear as a scum on the whey. Keep skimming this off into a fine wicker basket or a sterile muslin suspended over a colander. This is eaten very fresh so simply drain and chill.

Return to the Halloumi
When drained turn the curd out of the basket and cut into slices. Roll these in freshly chopped mint. Place them back in the whey to firm up further. There is no need for additional heat. When they float take them out. Make a brine by adding sufficient salt to the whey to float an egg (so that it shows about the area of a 10p piece). Take the egg out and put the cheeses in. They will keep in the brine for several months.

In the Middle East Halloumi is often grilled on a skewer over charcoal as part of a kebab.

COOKING WITH CHEESE
Many cookery books have sections on cheese and there are whole volumes on the subject so here I will only attempt to give a few basic recipes involving cheese and maybe one or two ideas for new ways of using it.

Mornay Sauce
This sauce, which is an adapted béchamel, is the basic cheese sauce for which there are many uses.
1 oz. (25g) butter
1 oz. (25g) flour
½ pint (225ml) hot milk
Grated cheese (Gruyère, Cheddar or Parmesan) amount very much
 depends on taste.
1 teaspoonful of made mustard
A little cayenne pepper.

Melt the butter, stir in the flour, let it bubble for a minute or two but not brown (this is a white roux). Stirring carefully, gradually incorporate the milk, returning to boil after each addition and stir well to absorb and cook flour. When all the milk has been added to form a smooth roux, add salt pepper and mustard. Let it simmer for 5 minutes to cook, *before* you add the cheese.

Cheese Soufflé
1½ oz. (40g) butter
1 oz. (25g) flour
½ pint (225ml) milk
3 oz. (75g) grated cheese
3 egg yolks
4 whites of egg
Salt and pepper

Prepare a soufflé dish by buttering liberally, coating with flour and shaking out. It is also an idea to place a 'collar' of greaseproof paper so that it extends about 2 in. (5cm) above the rim of the dish to support the soufflé as it rises. This can be removed before it is served.

Make a béchamel with the flour, butter and milk and add cheese. Season and remove from heat. Add the yolks one by one and leave in a warm place. Beat the egg white to a firm snow. Fold these quickly and evenly into the mixture with a metal spoon and bake for 20-25 minutes at 350°F (177°C, gas mark 4) until it has risen high and is brown. This is a very simple dish and the only disaster that can happen is that no one is ready to eat it.

Scrambled Eggs Brillat-Savarin
6 eggs
5 oz. (150g) grated Gruyère
2 oz. (50g) butter
Pepper, salt, croûtons

Beat eggs lightly and put on low heat with cheese, butter and pepper. Taste to see if salt is needed. Serve on toast or with croûtons as garnish or both.

Welsh Rarebit
8 oz. (225g) grated Cheddar cheese
1 oz. (25g) butter
1 teaspoonful of dry mustard
$\frac{1}{4}$ pint (150ml) beer or ale

Place all the ingredients in a heavy pan and blend thoroughly until melted. Pour over toast and grill until bubbling and golden. Serve with worcestershire sauce.

Croque-Monsieur
2 slices of bread per person
1 slice ham
1 thin slice Gruyère
$\frac{1}{2}$ oz. (12g) butter
$\frac{1}{2}$ tablespoonful of oil

Butter bread thinly and make a sandwich of the ham and cheese. Press firmly shut. Heat the butter and oil in a frying pan and when hot fry the sandwiches, turning carefully, on both sides.

Mozzarella in Carrozza
Mozzarella is the Italian cheese traditionally used in pizza. This name means mozzarella in a carriage and is a sort of Italian croque-monsieur.
2 slices of *thick* bread per person, shop sliced bread is much too thin.
2 eggs
Mozzarella cheese (or Bel Paese as a substitute)
Salt and pepper
Olive oil

Make thick sandwiches with the bread and cheese and, if necessary, fasten them with toothpicks. Beat the eggs in a large plate with salt and pepper and soak the sandwiches for about 15 minutes each side. Fry quickly in hot olive oil until golden brown, remove and drain thoroughly.

Cheese Semolina
French friends staying with us were surprised to see us eating hot

sweet semolina pudding. For them sweet semolina is eaten cold; hot, it is served with cheese ... and very good it is too.
1½ pints (275ml) milk
1 lb (450g) of cheese (or according to taste), grated
4 oz. (100g) semolina
Pepper to taste

Boil the milk and add semolina, stir until thick and smooth and then add most of the cheese (reserving some for top) and pepper. Turn out into an oven dish, cover top with grated cheese and brown under the grill.

Gougère
This is a sort of cheese choux paste, (the type used in éclairs) and is a bit tricky but worth trying.
6 oz. (175g) water or milk-and-water
6 oz. (175g) flour
2 oz. (50g) butter
4 eggs
3 oz. (75g) Gruyère cheese
Salt and pepper

Bring water or milk and water to the boil and then let it cool. Put in the butter cut in small pieces, a little salt and freshly ground pepper and bring quickly to boil so that the butter melts. Add the flour, stirring well until a thick smooth paste is obtained. Take off the heat and add the eggs one at a time, each one to be incorporated thoroughly before the next one is added. When the paste is smooth and shiny add the cheese cut in cubes (this is said to be important). Keep a tablespoonful back for finishing. When thoroughly melted, cool a little. Butter a baking sheet and make a ring of the paste on it with a well in the middle, then place reserved cheese on top. Cook for 35-45 minutes at 375°F (191°C, gas mark 5). Resist temptation to keep looking at it – it smells ready before it is. Test by pressing finger in centre of cake, it should be firm. A good dish hot or cold.

Fondue
There are a whole range of dishes which consist mainly of melted cheese with something dipped into it. These dishes have about them something of a festive air and the whole point of a fondue is that not

CHEESE-MAKING RECIPES

only is it a good meal but also it is fun. There are many recipes – this is a Swiss one, but you can adapt it and arrive at your own domestic one. You will need either a proper fondue set or a heavy pan and some long forks. The traditional pan is *caquelon*, which is kept hot over a spirit lamp. So long as you can devise a way of keeping it hot, any heavy pan will do.

1 clove garlic
3 oz. (75g) butter
4 tablespoonsful of flour
2 lbs (900g) cheese
1 pint (550ml) cider, beer or dry wine (for children use milk)
Salt, pepper

For an authentic flavour use Emmenthal or Gruyère cheese but any English hard cheese (including your own) makes a fondue – it will just have a different flavour. Rub inside the pan with garlic. The pan should be heavy. Melt the butter, stir in the flour and cook the white roux. Pour in cider or beer and simmer for 2 minutes. Stir in cheese, once again purists say cubed, not grated. Season lightly.

Have ready separate dishes of french bread, cauliflower florets, pieces of apple, carrot, gherkin and banana, to dip in.

Moitié-moitié is the name given to fondue made with half Gruyère and half Vacherin cheeses. Add the Vacherin only when the Gruyère has begun to melt.

There are almost as many different fondues as there are Swiss, Savoyard or Jurassian mountains and valleys.

Using the Whey

As a by-product of cheese-making you will have a lot of whey. Never waste this. It contains very valuable elements. Here are some possible uses.

1. *As stock feed.*

2. *As a drink.*
Not now very popular but at one time highly esteemed.

> 'Water and whey of drinks are first,
> They cool, dilute and quench the thirst'
>   Pope

The flavour of the whey will depend entirely on the curd from which it has drained. Here is the recipe for Green Whey.
8 oz. (225g) whey
Juice of ½ lemon
Pinch of salt
1 dessertspoonful of sugar

This must be prepared by taste. Add enough lemon just to give a slight aroma, the natural taste of the whey must not be swamped. Add only enough sugar to make palatable. Chill very thoroughly.

3. *Whey Toast*
1 large slice of white bread without crusts. 2 oz. (50g) whey. Butter as required. Dip bread into whey to moisten but not to make it soggy. Toast both sides and spread with butter. Try this with jam or under scrambled egg.

4. *As Curds and Whey*
This is not so much a way of using the whey as a dish involving whey.

5. *Whey Butter*
It takes 100 gallons of whey to produce 2 lbs (900g) butter so is of little relevance to the small scale producer. The cream is separated and it is made much as ordinary butter but needs extra washing.

6. *Whey Cheese*
In making Halloumi and Anari, one sort of whey cheese has been seen in which the albumin in the whey is flocculated. There is another type and this can be very useful if you or your family happen to like its rather strange taste. That is the Scandinavian whey cheese. It is not really a cheese at all for cheese is by definition made from curd and this substance is made entirely from whey.

Mysost Type Cheese. Heat the whey slowly in a large heavy pan. The object is to evaporate the water content and leave a brown caramel-like paste. When the whey has reduced considerably (to about ¼ original volume) cream can be added, this improves the consistency but alters the flavour a good deal, making it very fudge-like. It is definitely an acquired taste. (It has been compared with bad toffee, sweet manure, patent medicine, mouldy hay and tobacco.) In

Scandinavia it is almost the national cheese. It is marketed in blocks and very finely sliced pieces are eaten on rye bread.

Milk Surpluses
Cow's milk can be deep frozen. It may separate after a few months but can be run through a blender or used for cooking. The volume of space it takes up however, detracts seriously from the usefulness of the operation in comparison with e.g. making cheese from the milk and preserving it that way.

Goats milk can similarly be frozen and if the milk is needed for someone suffering from allergy or eczema there is a valid reason for so doing.

Containers

Cartons
Small Scale Supplies (see *Useful Addresses*) market 1 pint (550ml) goat's milk cartons which can be sealed with metal clips. A bench clip sealer is also required and they sell these as well.

5 oz. (150g) yogurt containers with snap on lids can be obtained from the same source. Waddingtons of Leeds (see *Useful Addresses*) are a direct source of cartons as are Bowaters (but Bowaters do not deal in small quantities). If you use these cartons either for your own use or for selling milk do make sure that they are correctly sealed. To seal them with staples is folly, they can rust, cause blood poisoning, fall into the milk and get swallowed. Proper packaging is always worthwhile; if you are selling goods the cost can be passed on to the consumer.

Plastic Bags
As an alternative to cartons, plastic bags, which can be closed with a heat sealing device are very suitable. They take up less room in the freezer and are considerably cheaper to buy. Their one disadvantage is that they are somewhat more fragile. The plastic can tear if it gets rubbed but properly handled they are a very good alternative. They are obtainable from Lakeland Plastics. (see *Useful Addresses*.)

Butter
Butter can be frozen and will keep for several months. It must be very well wrapped. Alternatively it can be potted.

Selling your Produce

People *do* sell Jersey cream and clotted cream from the farm gate, but the regulations are very stringent. If you are contemplating doing so get in touch with your Dairy Husbandry Advisory officer – each region has one and you can find the address either in your telephone directory or in the booklet 'At the Farmer's Service' which is available free from the Ministry of Agriculture publications department (see *Useful Addresses*). You will need to comply with a number of laws including The Food & Drugs Act 1955, the Milk and Dairies (General) Regulations 1959, The Cheese Regulations 1970, the Labelling of Food Regulations 1970. Copies are obtainable from H.M.S.O. Further your own County Council will need to know as will the Weights and Measures authorities. You will need to register with the Milk Marketing Board and then if your premises and methods comply you will be in business. It all sounds extremely daunting but people *do* do it, and have done so for centuries so do not let the red-tape deprive you of the right to sell from the farm gate if you can do so legally.

Goat produce is easier to market simply because the same stringent regulations do not apply. Nevertheless Public Health Authorities have the right to investigate your premises, standards etc. The National Dairy Goat Produce Association has been formed to help those who wish to market their produce (see *Useful Addresses*).

If you are selling any such produce it is a good idea to take out a public liability insurance, so that if anyone does suffer from your produce you are covered. Never use shoddy or second-hand packaging, this is a health risk as well as being bad business anyway. If your milk, cheese or yogurt is good it will find a ready market; health food shops and 'wholefood' shops are opening up by the score. Local pubs and restaurants will often buy home produced cheeses if they can be sure of a reliable and consistent supply.

At last people are seeking the original, the individual taste of country produce and the interesting craft of home dairying can provide not only good food for your table but some extra cash too. Time and trouble spent on presentation is never wasted, now more than ever is the moment when even large stores are eager to accept 'home produced' or small scale items – so good luck to you!

USEFUL ADDRESSES

Equipment
There are now several excellent stockists of the equipment needed by the small-scale producer. It is worthwhile, however, before sending off for catalogues, to pay a visit to your nearest farm suppliers. You will certainly be able to purchase such items as dairy detergent-sterilizer and worming tablets – at less cost than paying postage would entail.

Self-Sufficiency and Small-Holding Supplies, The Old Palace, Priory Road, Wells, Somerset BA5 1SY. Tel. Wells 72127.

Small Scale Supplies, Widdington, Saffron Walden, Essex CB11 3SP. Tel. Saffron Walden 40922. (They produce the excellent magazine *Practical Self-Sufficiency*.)

R.J. Fullwood & Bland Ltd, Ellesmere, Salop SY12 9DG. (Midget milking machines, electric cream separators, rennet.)

Gascoignes Ltd (Milking Division), Berkeley Avenue, Reading, Berks RG1 6JW (Miracle milking machines.)

J.J. Blow, Oldfield Works, Chatsworth Road, Chesterfield S40 2DJ. (Hand churns, 'Dairythene' buckets and churn brushes.)

Clares Carlton, Wells, Somerset BA5 1SQ. (Cheese record books.)

Astell Laboratory, 172, Brownhill Road, Catford, London SE6 2DL. (Lewis bottles, polythene starter bottles, thermometers, and Lloyd's acidimeters.)

Deva Bridge Ltd, PO Box 5, Stowmarket, Suffolk. (Yogurt kits.)

Tefal Housewares Ltd, Rivermeade, Oxford Road, Uxbridge. (Ice-cream makers.)

Robby Tanks, Cruwys Morchard, Tiverton, Devon (Home pasteurizers.)

Chris Hansen Laboratories Ltd, 476 Basingstoke Road, Reading RG2 0QL (Starters, rennet, annato.)

Divertimenti, 68/70 Marylebone Road Lane, London W1. (Shop selling a large range of home dairy equipment.)

Lakeland Plastics, 54 Alexandra Buildings, Station Precinct, Windermere, Cumbria (Plastic bags, heat sealing equipment.)

Waddingtons, 40 Wakefield Road, Leeds (Cartons and clips for milk.)

MAKING CHEESES, BUTTERS, CREAM AND YOGURT

Dairying Courses
Many agricultural colleges offer cheese-making courses as do some smallholders (advertised in *Practical Self-Sufficiency*, published by Broad Leys Publishing, Widdington, Saffron Walden, Essex CB11 3SP).

Mrs May, Priestlands Goat Farm, Claygate, Marden, Kent. (Basic and advanced cheese-making course.)

Farm Museums
Manor Farm Cogges, Nr Witney, Oxfordshire. (Arrange butter-making demonstrations in an Edwardian dairy.)

Easton Park Farm, Nr Wickham Market, Suffolk. (A detailed reconstruction of a Victorian dairy.)

'Curds & Whey', Dottens Farm, Baring Road, Cowes, Isle of Wight. (A modern farm giving talks on cheese-making and selling home-made cheeses.)

Information on Goats
The National Dairy Goat Produce Association, Golden Grove, Bishop's Castle, Shropshire. (Information on the standards and marketing of goat produce.)

The British Goat Society, Rougham, Bury St Edmunds, Suffolk, 1P30 9LJ. (Information about breeds of goats.)

FURTHER READING

A Book of Middle Eastern Food, Claudia Roden, (Penguin, London)
Food in England, Dorothy Hartley, (MacDonald & Jane, London)
Herdsmanship, R. Newman Turner, (Faber & Faber, London)
Indian Cookery, Balbir Singh, (Mills & Boon)

INDEX

Acidimeter (for cheese-making), 85
Almond Creams, 57
Anari, 113
Anchovy Butter, 74
Annatto, 95

Balkan Yogurt Cake, 45
Beestings (calf's milk), 37
    Cake, 38
Beurre Bercy, 73
    Blanc, 72
    Colbert, 73
    Manié, 75
    Maître d'Hôtel, 73
    Marchand de Vin, 72
    Noisette, 74
Black Butter, 75
Blancmange (Shape), 37
Book of the Farm, 67
Brandy Butter, 75
Brown Bread Cream, 54
Butter, colouring, 69
    Creams, 75-6
    faults with, 70-1
    flavouring, 72-6
    freezing, 119
    lactic, 68
    preserving, 71
    salting, 70
    sweet cream, 67
    to sweeten, 71
    washing, 69
Butterfat, 11, 12, 14, 17
Butter-making 67-71
    problems, 69
Buttermilk, 76-7
    scones, 76
Buytrose, 11

Caerphilly, 104
Cakik (cucumber salad), 43

Calf's milk (beestings), 37
    custard, 37
Caper Butter, 74
Carotene, 17
Cartons, 119
Casein, 11
Caseous, 11
Caudel, simple, 30
Cheddar, 106
Cheese, coagulation of, 83
    colouring of, 95
    consistency of, 83
    fat content of, 83
    fermentation of, 81-2
    fly, 103
    mite, 103
    presses, 88-9
    Semolina, 115-16
    Soufflé, 114
    starter, 40, 92-5
Cheese-making, faults with, 102-3
    history of, 78-81
Chenna, 44
Cheshire cheese, 104
Chessit and follower, 89-90
Churns (varieties of), 63-6
Clafoutis, 60
Clarified Butter, 75
Coeur à la Crème, 111
Colby, 104-5
Colwick, 105
Containers, 119
Cotherstone, 105
Cottage cheese, 96
Coulommier cheese, 97-9
Cream, clotted, 47, 49-52
    double, 47
    half, 47
    in sauces, 61
    pasteurization of, 49
    recipes, 52-62

separation of, 47-9
single, 47
sterilized, 47
whipping, 47, 49
Crema di Mascherpone, 112
Crème Brûlée, 56
   Caramel, 36
   Chantilly, 53
   Fraîche, 52
   Patissière, 36
Crémets d'Angers, 53
Crempog, 76
Croque-Monsieur, 115
Crowdie, 106
Cucumber Salad (cakik), 43
Cumberland Rum Butter, 75
Curd, 14, 15
   cutting knives, 90-92
   and whey, 77
Custards, 35, 56

Dairy equipment, 22-5, 26-7
   location of, 25-6
Derby cheese, 106
Double Gloucester, 107
Draining trays, 90

Egg Flip, 28
Equipment (for butter-making), 63-6
   (for cheese-making), 27, 84-93
Ewe's cheese, 112

Fluffin, 34
Fondue, 116
Fontainbleau, 52
Food in England, 78
Fore-milk, 20-21
Fromage Blanc, 111
Frumenty, 34

Garlic Butter, 74
Gougère, 116
Green Butter, 73

Halloumi, 112
Hartley, Dorothy, 78
Hasties, 35
Hatted Kit, 77

Haybox, 41
Herb Butters, 73-4
'Holder' method (of pasteurization), 16
'Hot iron' test (for cheese), 86
House fly (effect on cheese), 103

Ice-cream, 57-61
   chocolate, 60
   fruit, 59
   nut, 60
   vanilla, 59
Immos, 44
Incubation (for cheese culture), 94

Junket, 32

Kefir, 33
Koumiss, 32

Laban, 43
Lactobacillus acidophilus, 39, 40
   l. bifidis, 39
   l. bulgaricus, 39
lactose, 11, 12, 13
Lait du Poule, 28
Lebanie (Yogurt cheese), 46
Leicester cheese, 107
Lobster Butter, 74
London Syllabub, 31

Mastitis, 17, 21
Mexican Chocolate, 28
Milk and Brandy Punch, 30
Milk, Channel Island, 14
   composition of, 11
   condensed, 15
   dried, 15
   evaporated, 15
   ewes, 15
   goats, 12, 15, 16, 19
   homogenized, 14
   of Almonds, 31
   pasteurized, 14
   Punch, 30
   recipes, 28, 38
   selling of, 21, 23
   shakes, 28
   souring of, 15, 16

INDEX

South Devon, 14
sterilized, 14
stone, 23, 24
surpluses, 119
taints in, 18-19
UHT, 14
untreated, 13
Milking, 20-22
    area, 19-20
    machines, 23
Minerals, 12, 13
Moka, 60
Mon Ami, 55
Mont Blanc, 54
Montpellier Butter, 72
Mornay Sauce, 113
Moulds, 90
Mozzarella in Carrozza, 115
Muslins, 23
Mustard Butter, 74
Mysost Type Cheese, 118

Neufchatel, 112

Panir, 44
Party Egg Nog, 29
Pasteur, Louis, 16
Pasteurization, 16
Plastic bags (for freezing), 119
Pont L'Evêque, 111
Port-du-Salut, 110
Posset, simple, 29
    Pope's, 30
Protein, 12-13

Rennet, 33
Rice Pudding, 82, 92

Salep, 33
Sauce Messine, 61
    Mousseline, 61
Scrambled Eggs Brillat-Savarin, 114
Selling produce, 120
Serous, 11

Shape (Blancmange), 37
Shropshire Sage, 107-8
Smallholder's Cheese, 100-2
Soyer's Bread and Milk, 35
Stilton, 99-100
'Straw' test, 85-6
Stroganoff Sauce, 62
Syllabub, 55

Teat cup cluster, 23
    liners, 24
'Temperature' method (of pasteurization), 16
Thermometer (for cheese-making), 84
Tomato Butter, 74
Treacle Blancmange, 37
    Milk, 28
Tuberculosis, 11
Typhoid, 11

Ukranian Kasha, 45

Vitamins, 13, 14, 40

Water (in milk), 12, 13
Waterbath, 87-8
Wax (for coating cheese), 95
Welsh Rarebit, 115
Wensleydale, 108
Whey, 11, 15, 117
    butter, 118
    cheese, 118
    toast, 118
Whisky Cream Crowdie, 54
Wine Whey, 30
Worcester Butter, 74

Yeasts, 103
Yogurt Cheese (Lebanie), 46
    culture, 40, 41
    flavouring, 42-3
    recipes, 42-6
    starter, 40, 41
York/Cambridge cheese, 109